QUESTIONS OF THE DAY. NO. LVII.

THE PLANTATION NEGRO AS A FREEMAN

OBSERVATIONS ON HIS CHARACTER, CONDITION, AND PROSPECTS IN VIRGINIA

BY

PHILIP A. BRUCE

CORNER HOUSE PUBLISHERS

WILLIAMSTOWN, MASSACHUSETTS 01267

1970

CONTENTS.

INTRODUCTION.

THE Southern negro, both as a man and as a citizen, has been so often and so fully discussed, and from such a variety of standpoints, that it would seem almost impossible now for any new information to be produced, or any opinion advanced that would be likely to add much to the general knowledge of the problem which his presence creates, or to dispel any of the darkness that envelops his future. That his presence in the South constitutes a problem of the gravest importance is obvious to any one who has had an opportunity of examining closely the various tendencies of his nature and conduct in those rural communities in which individuals of his race form a large proportion or a great majority of the inhabitants.[1] It is in such communities as these that the observations embodied in this volume were made, these observations extending over a long series of years, but being entirely confined to the period that has elapsed since the war. It is only as a freeman that the negro has been presented to my view, for I have no distinct recollection of slavery as an institution ; it is only as he has been affected by the circumstances surrounding him since his emancipation that he is regarded

[1] The overwhelming majority of the Southern negroes are found in the rural districts, the number inhabiting the towns and cities being too small to exercise any material influence on the general destiny of their race.

in the following pages. I have sought to describe him in the light of that modification of his character which subsequent conditions have worked, as well as in the light of the resistance to these conditions which his ancestral traits are still making. The picture drawn will, no doubt, seem gloomy and repelling in its moral aspects. In reference to this, I will only say that I have stated my conclusions impartially and dispassionately, without any intention of improperly reflecting upon a population deserving of consideration in so many ways, and entitled to forbearance in all. If I have fallen into any mistake, it has been in applying to that population the common ethical standard by which the members of white communities are judged. I have been led to employ this standard not only because I believe it to be the only proper test, but also because I earnestly hope that a description of the moral, social, and political bent of the negroes, wherever they are found in a teeming mass, will quicken the efforts of those who are engaged in the task of improving them. No one can dwell for any length of time in those sections of the South where the members of that race predominate, without being animated by a strong desire that every means should be used to reform and elevate them, if not on their own account, then on account of the country which they inhabit. Patriotism steps in to inspire the wish, whether it would otherwise arise or not. I have been moved to write with unreserved freedom and candor, in order that there may be a clearer conception of the evils springing from the presence of the blacks, as well as a juster notion as to the nature of the remedies that should be adopted to remove these evils. There is much in the moral character of this people that is partially ascribable to the influences of slavery ; I have not touched at any length on these influences, because my aim has been to delineate the negro as he is, without reverting to the possible causes of his condition that are to be found in the past. Now that he is a freeman and a citizen, he must stand like the members of every other class, on his own individual merits, and according to these merits he must be estimated. An apology for his shortcomings on the score of slavery has no practical bearing now, except so far as it is calculated to diminish the discouragement which his moral deficiencies are apt to inspire. Every decade withdraws him still further from the transmitted spirit of the former régime ; every decade only removes a still greater number of the artificial props that have hitherto supported him. The truest lover of his country, as well as the most disinterested friend of the blacks, is he who will portray their character and depict their society, without partiality and without prejudice. It is difficult to understand how any one can contemplate in a narrow and illiberal way the questions involved in their numerical increase at the South, for these questions in reality touch every citizen, affect directly or remotely the interests of every community, and are as wide in their scope as the republic itself. Such questions come very closely home to the Southern people. Much as the subject of the negro has been discussed, that subject continues to be profoundly interesting to them, because it is so intimately associated with the welfare and prosperity of the section in which they live. In the light of this interest, which they share with the most thoughtful citizens in every other section of the Union, a further contribution to that discussion will, perhaps, be neither ill-timed nor useless.

The part of the South to which the observations re-

corded in these pages especially relate is that portion of
the Old Dominion which lies between the James River
and the northern boundary line of North Carolina, a
broad area of country which is locally designated as
Southside Virginia. It has long been known as one of
the most important tobacco regions of the United States,
every variety of that staple, with few exceptions, being
cultivated there ; for that reason, it was, before the late
war, the principal seat of the slave-holding interest in the
State, tobacco requiring in its production more arduous
and protracted labor than cotton. By the census of 1860,
there were 207,668 negroes in this section, a number that
had increased in 1880, after an interval of twenty years,
to 252,475, which is not very far from being one half of
the whole colored population of the commonwealth. In
many counties of Southside Virginia the blacks constitute two thirds of the inhabitants, this being strikingly
the case in the group that form the famous "black belt,"
which includes Amelia, Brunswick, Charlotte, Cumber-
land, Greensville, Mecklenburg, Nottoway, Powhatan,
Prince Edward, Prince George, Surry, and Sussex. In
Buckingham the negroes exceed the whites numerically
by two thousand ; in Lunenburg, by the same ; in South-
ampton, by three thousand ; in Dinwiddie, by four
thousand ; in Halifax by seven thousand. In Campbell
and Pittsylvania they have a majority in a combined population of 90,000. In all of these counties, which consist of a varied country of great extent, there are comparatively few school districts even, in which the whites
predominate over the blacks. The whole section is, in
fact, inhabited by large communities of negroes, in which
their characteristics are developed in entire freedom
from the pressure of any influences except those that

emanate from themselves. Nowhere can the tendencies of the race as a mass be studied to more advantage; and it is only as a mass that I have sought to present the individuals of that race in this volume. For this reason, the observations are generalized, as a rule, and, except in the instance of the chapters on the material condition of colored laborers, without special local details. While the scope of these observations is more or less locally restricted, yet I believe that they will be found to be applicable, so far as they bear on the moral and social tendencies of the negro, to all parts of the South in which the black population forms large communities, which withdraws it from the influence of the whites, and exposes it only to the influences that arise in its own society. The members of that population have recently emerged from the same state everywhere; their homogeneity as a people has always been remarkable at every period of their history, and wherever they have been observed. The local circumstances surrounding them in the southern counties of Virginia, do not differ from those that hedge them about in the cotton region; Southside Virginia is, in fact, only the beginning of the black belt that runs as far to the southwest as Texas. What is true of the negroes in one division of this belt is very likely to be true of them in every other, only that in South Carolina, Mississippi, and Louisiana, the condition of the race is still more degraded, and the problem which that condition creates more difficult of solution, on account of the numerical disproportion between the whites and blacks throughout the whole of these commonwealths, and not, as in Virginia, in isolated parts alone. PHILIP A. BRUCE.

RICHMOND, VA., Nov. 1, 1888.

THE PLANTATION NEGRO AS A FREEMAN.

I.

PARENT AND CHILD.

OF all the domestic influences at work among the plantation negroes of Virginia wherever they are gathered together in large communities of their own, the most important
in its scope, on the whole, is that which emanates from
the relation of parent and child. It is to this relation
that the attention of an observer of their society is first
directed, because, of the various elements that enter into
that society, it is likely to throw most light upon the
future of the race, even if it does not give the clearest in-
dication of its present moral and social condition. How
far does the parental authority supply the discipline that
was enforced by the slaveholder? And to what extent
does it foster a spirit of self-control in the masses of
those who, in time, will shape the public sentiment of
their people? If the answer to these questions is unfavorable to this relation, to what can we look to cultivate
that spirit, without which neither the young nor the old
are capable of usefulness or worthy of esteem? A
search in other directions is soon discovered to be vain.

If the parental authority is powerless, then there is no other form of authority to take its place.

Turning for a moment to the character of the negro as a parent when a slave,[1] we find that the authority to which he had to submit had a favorable effect on his relation to his children. The mere fact that he was under a vigilant and energetic guardianship himself inclined him to restrain them far more than he would have done if he himself had not been governed at all. The spirit that was imparted to him by his situation in life he communicated to them, and he was further stimulated to confine them within proper bounds by his anxiety not to incur on their or his account the displeasure or censure of their master. If he found that he was unable to check them, then it was only necessary for him to ask that master to interfere, and his request was promptly complied with. As soon as they arrived at the age of intelligence, they themselves saw that they were as much and as constantly under the rigorous supervision of their owner as of their parents, and, in many instances, more so, and this double force of authority fully controlled them in their daily life. Thus the spirit of obedience and restraint was inculcated in them from their earliest years, and whether supine or restive under restriction, they knew that it was impossible to escape from it. While the power of slavery thus manifested did much to complement and strengthen the parental authority and even to supply it when it was wanting, it did little to animate the father and mother with a desire to improve their children morally, because it did nothing to incite them to improve themselves. Neither of the parents

[1] All references to slavery are inferential and speculative, not being based on my personal observation or experience.

was capable of instructing their children in the simplest
moral principles ; they were either unenlightened themselves, or if they did comprehend the ethical difference
between a virtue and a vice, they were generally unin-
formed as to the proper manner of teaching it ; and
their cabin, in consequence, was an unwholesome atmosphere for a youthful nature to draw its first breath in
after it had begun to observe its surroundings. In that
atmosphere the disposition of the child expanded in
harmony with the low instincts that had come down to
him through so many ages ; slavery stepped in to restrain these instincts when uncontrollable otherwise, although it did nothing to eradicate them and to substitute
pure and honorable impulses for them. If that power
which the master's property in his slave child gave him
the right to exercise, with a view to governing him,
either directly or by sustaining the parental authority,
had not been brought to bear for that purpose, then
practically the child would have been left to follow his
worst inclinations, since his father and mother were themselves too destitute of all proper knowledge or feeling to
teach him at the time that they punished him, if they
punished him at all when he did wrong. The discipline
of slavery was therefore advantageous in a repressive
way to the child, selfish and ruthless as it was too often.

In none of the domestic relations has the influence of
emancipation been more obvious in its working than in
that of parent and child, but the result might have been
predicted by any one who was familiar with this relation
under the former system, as well as with the general disposition of the negro himself. The parental authority
is now much laxer than it used to be, inasmuch as it is
no longer supported by all the power of the slaveholder.

Even if, in any instance, a father and mother were to desire to instil a spirit of self-restraint into their children, they would not be led to seek, when necessary, the assistance of their former master, who is now their employer, and who never assumes the right to intervene, unless the heedlessness or depravity of the children is displayed in injuring, destroying, or purloining his property. He has no longer authority enough to insist upon order and discipline in the family life, or to compel parents to prevent their offspring from running wild, like so many young animals. Even when he feels any interest in their moral education, irrespective of their connection with the government of his own estate, he finds it impossible to come near enough to them to win and hold their attention, for child and parent alike shrink from association with him. His advances are not cordially met. However keen his sense of moral responsibility, therefore, and however earnestly he may wish to prosecute a plan of moral education among the children of his laborers, he runs upon an almost insurmountable obstacle in his path at the very beginning, and he is generally discouraged from going any further. As far, therefore, as he is concerned, the children of the new generation receive no moral instruction at all. Under the old system, the ladies of his family often instituted Sunday-schools, to teach the young slaves the leading principles of the Christian faith, as well as general rules of good conduct; but this custom, which was the source of much benefit to the pupils, has fallen into disuse ; and as there are now no points of contact between the home life of the cabin and that of the planter's residence, no social or moral influence of any kind emanates from his domestic circle to enlighten the minds of the children who live on his estate.

I have already referred to the moral deficiencies of the parents when slaves. On the whole the parents of the present day are still more imperfect as ethical teachers and exemplars, because greater unsteadiness and laxness of conduct prevail among them under the freedom of the new régime than was observed under the strictness of the old. They are now at liberty to act upon all the impulses of their nature, these impulses being too often censurable as violating the rules of propriety and morality, or if not, then probably originating in an ignorance and carelessness that are as injurious in their consequences as depravity itself. It is too much to expect that parents, trained as the negroes have been, will be deeply interested in the moral condition of their children. Apart from any apology that can be offered in their behalf, it is undeniable that they either do not feel any solicitude about that condition at all, or do not feel it to the necessary degree. The average father and mother are morally obtuse and indifferent, and at times even openly and unreservedly licentious. Their character is such, by the force of nature or circumstances, that they have no just conception of the parental obligation or the onerous duties that it should lay upon them in the course of their daily lives. The children have come into the world by the operation of an instinct, and the burden which their rearing imposes is borne as thoughtlessly as that instinct itself was indulged. It is one of the most notable traits of the individual of the race that he does not look forward when his own interests would seem to require him to do so, and it is not to be supposed that his mind would turn to the future more readily for sake of his offspring, even if he were capable of appreciating the effect of early training on the whole tenor of after-life. He is not likely to act in one way with the young and in another with himself. In both cases his thoughts do not wander beyond the present. For sake of personal convenience merely, he is compelled to enforce a certain measure of discipline in his household, but it is, as a rule, done in a way that deprives it of an elevating influence. In neither of the parents, indeed, when it becomes necessary to rebuke or chastise their children, in order to insure a mere temporary good, do we generally find such deportment as will strike home a lesson that will redound to the permanent welfare of mind and heart by accustoming both to the pressure of steady but reasonable restraint. In only too many instances the tendency of the parents is to punish a slight indiscretion and to overlook a serious offense altogether, the usual consequence of which is, that the seeds of demoralization are sown in the receptive intelligence of their offspring at the hearth, where those lessons only should be taught which bear in after-life that noble fruit that separates a civilized human being from a grovelling beast.

As a rule, the negroes are not unkind in their general bearing as parents, since they are to a certain extent a genial and amiable people ; harshness and severity on their part proceed as much from mere impulsiveness as from a determination to be brutal and merciless. They frequently speak in a loud and threatening way to their children, and are often rough and cruel ; but observing their behavior for a considerable length of time, they are gentler, on the whole, than would have been anticipated of the members of a race that has always shown so little ability to use any form of power with wisdom and moderation. The principal ground for criticism in their intercourse with their offspring is, that they are not discrimi-

nating in their treatment, and not able to pursue any
course of conduct permanently, however necessary that
course may be ; an inability to follow out a single plan of
action for any length of time being one of the most striking
characteristics of their race. To keep a careful guard
over their children would be vexatious and tedious, as it
would require prolonged watchfulness and ceaseless attention to the smallest details. All this is foreign to the temper
of the negro, however excellent his intentions as a parent
might be. His nature is careless and indifferent ; he is
too capricious to persist in the same line of deportment,
and too shifting and irresolute in his purposes to interest
himself continuously in any one thing. The children of
the most respectable parents suffer in consequence, being
allowed to grow up without steady instruction in lessons
of propriety and morality, and to that extent to mature
in a state of nature, their original characters expanding
in accord with their inherent bent, unmodified by any
form of continuous training.

In one respect, however, the parents do show a marked
interest in the condition of their children ; they are anxious that the latter shall attend school, and always require
them to do so, unless the children cannot be dispensed
with about the house. In this the parents are governed
by several motives, and the advantage of educating their
sons and daughters for their own individual welfare in
life has perhaps less weight in the premises than other
reasons. The negro attaches an almost superstitious
value to such instruction ; he exalts the idea as if it were
that of a fetich ; it calls up a vague conception to his
mind that is pregnant with manifold but ill-defined benefits. At heart he believes that illiteracy is the principal
cause of the negro's social inferiority to the white man,

and he attributes to school instruction a marvellous power of removing this inferiority. He looks upon education, therefore, as a means of bringing his offspring, and through his offspring himself and his race, nearer to the social position of white people ; and he is actuated more by this sentiment on the whole than by a lively concern in the development of the mind of the child irrespective of the latter's relations with society at large.[1] Attendance upon school is perhaps beneficial to that child in the physical restraint to which it forces him to submit for the time being, but unfortunately the annual session does not extend over many months, and, furthermore, the scholars are withdrawn at an age when they are most impatient of constraint, and, consequently, when they stand peculiarly in need of the strictest discipline. They probably do not remain long enough to receive any general impression that will affect them throughout their future. The elementary knowledge which they acquire there is undoubtedly useful to them ; but the confinement of the school, so far from cultivating steadiness of character, seems to make them more eager to shake off all restriction as they grow older ; it certainly does not cause them to be less restive under the reins of the parental authority and less determined to escape from it as soon as they can.

There is little in that general society in which the children move, and of which they must take the form and pressure, to foster self-repression in their natures. Even if the domestic life of the cabin was as pure and elevating in its influence as it should be, then the spirit

[1] The importance which the negro attaches to education is also due, in some measure, to that imitative spirit which leads him to adopt so many of the customs of the whites.

of the community around them would do much to lessen
the beneficial effect of that influence. Few lessons are
to be learned in this atmosphere that inculcate propriety
of conduct and refinement in behavior ; on the contrary,
the child is too apt to learn there much that is calculated
to make him dishonest, much that encourages him to
give full rein to his various impulses and passions, and
thus to defy the restraining force of every right principle. In short, that unwholesome atmosphere is likely to
give such a tone to the child's mind that it is impossible
for him to lead a strictly upright life when he arrives at
maturity. Each community is but an aggregation of
ignorant homes, and each home is but a circle of thoughtless individuals. Far too many members of the older
generations set a demoralizing example, by showing little
appreciation in word and action alike for order, cleanliness, temperance, continence, veracity, and integrity.
The persons to whom the children should look up for
guidance and instruction, and in whose footsteps they
should be able to follow safely, too often inspire them
only with a more capricious and restless spirit. The
consequence is that those who should be the hope of
their race as the future representatives of its capacity, its
industry, and its virtue, promise to be less respectable
than their fathers, who were trained in the harsh school
of slavery. The general freedom has fostered a growing
impatience of restraint in the young. As soon as a youth
reaches the age of seventeen or eighteen, he begins to
chafe even under the lax parental authority ; every kind
of discipline galls him beyond endurance ; a settled
occupation is especially obnoxious and distasteful to
him, as he shrinks from an uninterrupted employment of
his energies. He is assured that he can earn a liveli-

hood without difficulty by casual and temporary contracts, and, therefore, he is anxious to confine himself to intermittent and irregular labor. The planters are so well aware of this inclination on his part that they are indisposed to engage him by the year, since he is not the less likely to slip away without warning, because he is still under the guardianship of his parents. Whoever among them gives him work places little reliance upon his promise to adhere to the terms of the agreement into which his father or mother may have entered, in his behalf, as there are no secondary means of enforcing the stipulations. The promptings of self-interest, idleness, or caprice will cause him to throw the hoe down in the fields and depart without serving any notice on his employer or without even informing his parents. As it is necessary for the security of certain crops that there should be a full force of laborers to work them at stated seasons, or manipulate them after they have been gathered and stored away in the barns, this unsteadiness and unreliability always do great harm if displayed at a critical hour. They cast a dark shadow over the prospects of the generation of negroes who have been brought up wholly under the influence of the new order of things.

In justice to the parents it must be said that they are very much opposed to the unsteady and roving disposition of their sons, although it is largely ascribable to their defective training ; but this opposition is not based upon sentimental reasons alone. To them the wages of their children properly belong until the latter come of age or marry. As it is, the parents have to bear the expense and incur the trouble of bringing up their sons only to see them break away for unknown parts, just at the time when they are old and strong enough to assist in eking out the support of the family by the money which they can earn by working in the fields.

The girls, on the other hand, are more easily managed, after a certain age, than the boys, because more amenable to physical restraint. The character of their sex puts a check upon their conduct in certain respects in which their brothers are most ungovernable ; in other words, they are less restive, because they are weaker and more timid. Necessarily they are not so much at liberty to shape their lives as they please as they approach maturity, and even if they had that inclination to roam which is shown by the boys, which they have not, it would not be in their power to gratify it. The relation between the girls and their fathers and mothers is gentler and more intimate, and as they are very useful in the household they are more highly valued and appreciated. Whatever wages they can earn belong to their parents. They can take no part in the roughest labor of the plantations, but at certain seasons, when the wheat harvest, for instance, is in progress, or the corn is being planted, or the tobacco stripped, many of them are regularly employed, and are paid well for their work. These are then found in the fields or barns at all hours of the day, and, to the extent of their physical strength, are as good hands as males of the same age. During the greater portion of the year, however, all of the girls are entirely disengaged, this long interval being spent in idleness or in assisting in the ordinary domestic routine of the cabin. Unfortunately, their mothers do not endeavor to teach them, systematically, those moral lessons that they peculiarly need as members of the female sex ; they learn to sew in a rude way, to wash, to iron, and to cook, but no principle is steadily instilled that makes them solicitous and resolute to preserve their reputations untarnished. Chastity is a virtue which the parents do not seem anxious to foster and guard in their daughter ; she has no abiding sense of personal purity in consequence, and the anticipation of the possible consequences of indiscretion does not appear to intervene to influence her to be circumspect in her behavior. The truth is that the only very serious consequence is physical, there being unhappily no stern sentiment even in her immediate family to condemn her. This looseness in the sexual relations does not lower her general disposition as much as might be supposed, for she is remarkable for a certain cheerfulness of spirit and amiability of temper that partially redeem her from the charge of occasional incontinence. In those other essentials of character that are the basis of esteem, and which should be enforced upon the consideration of children, male and female alike, the daughter is, as a rule, as undeveloped as the son ; and not unnaturally, since the usual examples of her own sex that come within the daily range of her observation, even in the precincts of her father's dwelling, are not such as to lead her to cultivate these traits to a considerable degree.

The intercourse between parents and children, after the latter have established homes and have families of their own, is not, as a rule, very intimate and constant, even when they live quite near together, but nevertheless the relation is not ignored. The negro is often cruel and generally callous, but still he has more warmth of heart than is usually found in individuals of other races equally ignorant, and while it is very improbable that he will inconvenience himself or sacrifice his interests to serve father or mother when the latter are embarrassed, yet he will show occasionally that he is not unmindful of their existence. It must be recollected in his favor that he has a heavy burden to carry in supporting his own children ; all that he can earn is thus expended, and therefore, even though he had the proper impulse, he could give but little material assistance to his parents if the latter were to seek it. The life which the members of both sexes lead, whether idle or laborious, is not such as to foster in their dispositions the growth of any kind of sentimentality, and it is not surprising that it should weaken and even destroy the filial tie altogether. If they ever dwell upon the past, their memories of their early years in the cabin would not, perhaps, arouse an emotion of filial gratitude, but this does not color their view of their relation to their parents in after-life at all. Their thoughts rarely revert to what has gone before, of their own accord ; even if the contrary were true, many would probably recall a harsh parent with as much honor as a kind and gentle one, for there is nothing that the average negro seems to respect so much as force, whether unscrupulous or not. The freedmen of the present day do not disclose by their bearing toward a former master who conducted himself with extreme harshness and injustice to them when slaves that they resent the rough and unprincipled usage to which they were then compelled to submit. Among the white men who are most popular with the negroes are those who used to have this evil reputation as slaveholders ; and so it is with a father and mother who were severe to their children when young. If the children neglect their parents, it is because they are oblivious of the filial obligation, and not because they are moved by a sense of injury ; and if their parents had heaped upon them every benefit, the children would probably be equally as indifferent. They do not always think that natural duty alone should prompt them to be attentive and useful to their parents whenever they can be ; nor do the parents on their side confidently expect to receive any help from their offspring, and if pinched in old age by extreme poverty they are less inclined on the whole to appeal to a son or daughter, however prosperous and unhampered, than to the planter who owned them before they were freed.   It is not until the last scene in the humble drama of their lives is reached that their children are invariably interested in their fate.   The sensibilities of the former are touched at once by the prospect of the early death of father or mother, even if they had felt no special concern about the temporary condition of either.   Every superstitious emotion in their breasts is aroused, and they display a morbid solicitude that assumes the form of the most violent grief when the parent finally dies.   The intensity of their sorrow is expressed in many ways, even if it had happened that they had abandoned the dead parent altogether before his or her last illness ; but this is only one of the numerous inconsistencies that distinguish the negro in every relation of life ; for he flies from one extreme to another so fast that we condemn and praise him, despise and pity him, like and dislike him, all at the same instant of time.

II.

HUSBAND AND WIFE.

PASSING to the relation of husband and wife, and incidentally to the more general relation of the sexes, I enter upon the examination of that part of my subject in which the plantation negro appears in the most unfavorable light, and which, therefore, cannot be discussed with freedom and accuracy without some appearance of harshness and cruelty. When he has an opportunity of gratifying his physical appetites, which are the more vigorous and impetuous the more feeble his intellect, he generally acts as if he had no conscience at all, and no fear, either of the serious consequences which his thoughtlessness may inevitably bring upon him ; his mind being so little able to form any just notion of these consequences, however grave, that he does not seem even to anticipate or calculate them. He gives way to his lowest physical propensities with as much mental serenity and self-abandonment as if they were innocent, although he may lay himself open thereby to very severe punishment. Indeed, the plantation negro is as much a child of nature now, however civilizing the influences that surround him, as if he had just been transported from the shores of his original continent. He apparently sees no immorality in doing what nature prompts him to do, whether he thus encroaches upon the absolute rights of others or not, for differences of title in those things which he

believes were created for all are not generally accepted
by him as adjudicated facts ; as a rule, he bears himself
towards such kinds of property as if there were no differences of ownership in them whatever. In the sexual
relations this insensibility and want of self-control are
exhibited to a very remarkable degree, for the procrea-
tive instinct being the most passionate that nature has
implanted in his body, it is unscrupulous in proportion.
Before it all the barriers which society has raised in the
instance of the white race, and with which it also endeavors to restrain the negro, go down as if they had no
power of thwarting his determination to gratify it.

Slavery certainly transmitted no influence to the present day that is calculated to moderate this instinct. That
system debased both man and woman by making true
marriage impossible, and in doing this it tempted both
sexes to revert to the natural relations of mere temporary
impulse and convenience. Continence and chastity could
not well be fostered and encouraged under it, as it was
opposed, in its first principles, to wholesome sentiment in
the family, and even to the existence of home itself,
which is the only fortification against promiscuous intercourse. However faithfully both members of the couple
might observe the marital obligations, their union could
amount only to a passing arrangement as long as their
owner had the power to sell either at any moment that
his interests moved him to do so. The possibility of
such rupture, followed by a final separation, was enough
in itself to weaken, or at least to embitter, the relation,
however firmly cemented apparently by affection and the
birth of children. Marriage under the old régime was
very like unlawful cohabitation under the new, only that
the master, by the power he had, compelled the nominal

husband and wife to live together permanently. They were not allowed to fly apart as they wished, and to assume a similar relation with other persons ; an ordinary regard for public opinion, or the mere necessity of maintaining order and discipline on his estate causing the planter to prevent this as far as he could, whether he was indifferent to it on the score of personal responsibility or not.

Although the institution of slavery did nothing to raise the dignity of marriage or to improve the relation of the sexes, it restricted illicit commerce among the negroes in some measure, because it restrained their general conduct. Before emancipation they had far less liberty of action in every way, necessarily ; they were not permitted then to associate in that unembarrassed fashion which their social and cheerful dispositions preferred, and which, now that they are free, they cultivate so assiduously and with so much pleasure. On the contrary, all their movements were then closely watched, and whether innocent or not, were followed with more or less suspicion. They were especially discouraged from wandering about much at night or mingling in large congregations ; thus their opportunities of falling into lewd habits were diminished, although the inclination to do so remained unchanged. The personal independence of the present day shows how powerful this inclination really was, in spite of the check that was put upon it by the systematic repression of slavery. It is not now reined in by circumstances at all, and the consequence is that it is gratified to such a degree that lasciviousness has done more than all the other vices of the plantation negroes united, to degrade the character of their social life since they were invested with citizenship. It is in this

direction that they seem to be tending most certainly
to a state of nature, and many influences are hasten-
ing the event. In the first place, they show a disposition to withdraw as far as possible from white
people, and to ignore the social laws of the latter, which
signifies their complete removal from the pressure of a
wholesome public sentiment ; in the second place, the
increasing restlessness of the individual negro causes
him to entertain a growing feeling of opposition to regular marriage, since it compels him to settle in one spot,
and imposes on him the necessity of supporting wife and
children. As long as he can form an illicit connection
for whatever length of time he chooses, he is not anxious to purchase a license, for this will fix a permanent
obligation upon him. The very cost of it, small as it is,
is an obstacle in the way of a legal union. If an annual
poll tax of one dollar will disfranchise a great many
negroes in every community by their inability to pay it,
the expense of marriage licenses will virtually prevent
others, so improvident is the character of the race, from
entering into the bonds of lawful matrimony ; or it will
at least prompt them to dispense with the license altogether as practically unnecessary.

The general incontinence of the negroes is very much
increased, too, by the fact that intrigue is one of the few
amusements which they have to quicken their lives. It
gives a savor to a flat existence passed in the midst of
the most secluded surroundings which it would not otherwise have ; and it is on this account, as well as because
they are naturally genial, that they celebrate their various entertainments and reunions with so much spirit.
These are frequently distinguished for low debauchery,
which encourages a course of subsequent intercourse and

association that breaks down the last barrier between the sexes, the effect being peculiarly demoralizing to the character of the women, who properly should be bulwarks of sobriety and conservatism to the society in which they move, whereas they are in general the floodgates of the corrupting sexual influences that are doing so much to sap and destroy it. The number of illegitimate children born to unmarried negresses is becoming greater every year, but this, instead of being a lasting stain on their reputations or a stumbling-block in the path of their material thrift, is an advantage when regarded from a practical point of view. If these children have come to an age when they are old enough to work, then they constitute a valuable dowry to whoever marry their mothers, such women occupying somewhat the position of widows with considerable property at their command, which they confer absolutely upon their husbands at the hour of marriage. In reality, a life of gallantry on the part of the females before that hour, whether it has its consummation in natural children or not, cannot be said to jar upon the sensibilities of the men in general, for they have apparently no sense of delicacy here. As a rule, they marry the most indiscreet of the other sex with as much unconscious satisfaction as the purest, and, on the whole, they are not as scrupulous as they should be as to whether they themselves or their intimate friends were parties to the antenuptial sexual irregularities of their wives. This state of mind on the part of the men with respect to the conduct of the women they marry, is very injurious to the moral tone of the unmarried women, for it removes the most powerful influence that could be brought to bear to make them prudent, inasmuch as the thoughtless and

wanton can secure husbands with the same ease as the
virtuous and circumspect. A plantation negress may
have sunk to a low point in the scale of sensual
indulgence, and yet her position does not seem to
be substantially affected even in the estimation of the
women of her own race, who, it would be supposed, if
we followed the analogy of women of all other races
wholly or partially civilized, would be even unjustly
severe on her contempt for decency. In those numerous
quarrels that agitate the intercourse of the plantation
women, one who is peculiarly open to reproach on account of her lewdness, is more frequently reviled for the
color of her skin than made the target of the foulest epi-
thet that can be launched at a woman. The truth is
that neither the women nor the men as a mass look upon
lasciviousness as impurity, and, therefore, it is not a
ground of rebuke or a subject for gibes or sneers, or a
justification for an assumption of superiority in those
who are comparatively chaste. This freedom of physical
commerce is regarded as a matter of course by the great
majority of the members of both sexes, unless, in some
special case, it results in a conflict of claims ; then it
frequently leads to crime in the first moments of violent
anger, but rarely if the object of that anger can escape
until the gust of passion has blown over. Far more
often, however, it is simply a cause of the most extravagant verbal engagements, that terminate peaceably when
the power of lung and tongue have been exhausted,
which only happens generally after an extraordinary
length of time has elapsed ; familiar and intimate relations are then resumed, to be amicably maintained until
a new occasion for complaint has arisen.

Marriage, however solemnly contracted and however

ite families apparently do nothing but dawdle. She
encouraged in this view by her husband, although he
ereby increases his own burdens ; for he considers it
proper for his wife to abandon her fireside to work
th the plantation laborers. When the married women
e observed thus engaged it is an evidence that their
milies are pinched by a degree of poverty that over-
des inclination as well as custom. This occurs with
mparative infrequency, however, since they are pro-
ded with all that they need by their husbands alone,
ho also do all the heavy or troublesome jobs about the
bins, such as digging the gardens, chopping the wood,
d weeding the patches of corn which they are allowed
till. Under circumstances so favorable to their physi-
l ease and mental tranquillity, the wives have little to
ccupy their attention. They do not go abroad much
vary their life ; indeed, the majority become so indo-
nt that they rarely move beyond their own thresholds,
onfining their visiting during the week to the different
ouses of the immediate neighborhood in which they
well. On Sunday, however, many are more inclined to
all on friends and acquaintances who reside at a much
reater distance from them, and they make this the occa-
ion for parading their finery. This feminine love of
ress is shared by them all, however ignorant or poor,
ut they show, not unnaturally, a keener appreciation of
ay splendor of hue than excellence of texture ; the
more pronounced and glaring the color, in fact, the
more elegant it seems to their uncultivated taste. When
thus arrayed, their satisfaction reaches the highest point
of self-contentment, which is exhibited in a complacency
of bearing as amusing as it is innocent. Under such trivial
circumstances as these the negro's mental incongruity and

public the religious ceremony sanctioning it, does not
wholly hamper the sexual liberty of either of the parties.
The wife, as a rule, is as innocently unconscious as the
husband that both have entered into a mutual pledge to
be faithful to the vows that they have pronounced. To
them, the ceremony is a form which sentimentally means
little, and practically signifies only that the woman shall
attend to all household duties and the man shall
work and support the family. Very unfortunately, this
view is even held by those who are regarded as the
spiritual leaders and exemplars of their race. Many of
the plantation preachers frequently offend against the
sacredness of their own marriages and the marriages of
members of their flocks, and instead of following that
course of propriety which their position requires that they
shall follow, they too often employ their commanding
influence to corrupt and lead astray. So leniently are
violations of the marriage oaths regarded by the negroes,
that divorce is a remedy to which they rarely have recourse.[1] The process is so expensive that few could
bear the cost except by stinting themselves and hoard-
ing their wages, but if their improvidence did not debar
them from turning to it, or if the advantages of the process could be obtained free, they would probably not
utilize it, for they are as a class quite insensible to that
principle of honor and self-respect which would lead a
sensitive husband or wife to discard a partner as person-
ally offensive because indifferent to the marital obligation of chastity. What is considered to be an imperative
ground for divorce even among the most uneducated
whites, rarely induces the plantation negro couple to

[1] No instance of such a divorce in the rural districts has fallen
within the scope of my own personal knowledge.

separate either for a short or a long time.   However gross the immoral act, it generally occasions only a flurry of passionate anger against the third person who is a party to it, with husband or wife.   Against the husband himself or the wife, as the case may be, no permanent feeling of resentment seems to be felt.

The instance very frequently occurs of a negro who has deserted his wife in one county, getting, by false statements, a license to marry in another county, and there establishing a new home with as much coolness as if he had been single when he obtained the second license ; but so accustomed are the whites to the sexual freedom of their former slaves that when it comes to their ears that a certain negro who resides in their vicinity has two wives to whom he is legally bound, living, the rumor, however capable of substantial proof, is almost always winked at or not considered worthy of investigation.   A criminal action for bigamy is far rarer than a civil action of divorce in the contemporary history of the race, although a legal basis for it can be so often laid.   Even when a marriage is hedged about with all the required forms of law and religion, it is difficult for the guardians of the peace to look upon its illegal violation as a criminal offense, so lightly and thoughtlessly do the blacks themselves regard the moral obligations of the tie.

The marriages that take place are generally contracted quite early in the lives of the parties to them, for the young men having no capital but their physical strength, and not expecting to have any other, are in as good a position to support a family when they reach the age of twenty-one as they are when much older.   There has not been sufficient accumulation of property by the negroes

who are somewhat advanced in year
them more eligible in the point of m
are younger.   The teachers in the
thought to be, on the whole, the most
because they are in receipt of salarie
mous as compared with the wages of
in the fields, or even a house serva
they are men of social eminence amo
their race.

The weddings are celebrated qui
boisterous gayety and homely pomp,
dancing that distinguish them being pr
break, when the guests reluctantly d
that follows marriage would seem to l
factory to the wife than to the husb
upon it is the signal to her to leave off
The home into which she is introduced
fortable than the cabin of her parents
was recently led to assume another r
this time forward her existence is freer
fore she was often compelled to take p
tions of the plantation at certain seaso
onerous tasks in the domestic manageme
dwelling were put on her.   Now she is n
be thus employed.   As a married woman
a degradation to cultivate the fields, an
duties are so light, until her children
when they can relieve her altogether, t
give no trouble.   Practically, therefore,
of her married life, even in the beginni
idleness.   She is disposed to look upon
that becomes her, both because it is v
itself and because the female members of

dull sense of the fitness of things are apparent. A gaudy bonnet jauntily set upon the head of the wearer, though the rest of her apparel may be unusually plain, titillates her vanity as pleasurably, and causes her to walk with as much stateliness, as if all her different articles of clothing were in keeping with the one piece of ornament, and an equally delighted state of feeling is raised by a still more insignificant bit of personal decoration, she not being aware that there is any thing out of harmony in her appearance.

The average wife has no keen appreciation of cleanliness. This she discloses not only in her own person, but also in the interior of her home, over which, as a wife and mother, she has absolute control to arrange the numerous objects and to preserve the whole in such condition as she chooses. The great majority of cabins disclose few evidences of refinement in the nature of her who should be the genius of the best influences of the household. The truth is, that the wife is inferior to the husband in many of the qualities of her character, and this is observed not only in the domestic but also in the general relations of life. She is more unbridled, for instance, in consequence of the more independent existence she leads as an individual who is not expected to do any thing that demands much exertion and self-denial. She is really under the pressure of very little, if any, restraint. Her husband, as an employee who must conciliate the good-will of the planter for whom he works and submit to all that is required of him, is far from being at liberty to act as he pleases ; his poverty puts a check upon his natural inclinations to a very important degree. But this is not the position of the wife, who is supported not by her own energy but by the energy of her husband, to whom she looks alone for a livelihood, and it is only rarely that she comes in contact with the landholder from whom the bread that sustains the lives of her family is indirectly gotten.   She is altogether removed, therefore, from any repressive influence which the whites might exercise over her on close association.

While in many instances the husband roughly domineers over the wife, yet, as a rule, the latter holds the reins of domestic power, and is fully able to defend herself, or even commit an assault when his bearing seems to justify it.   The shrewish temper and licentious tongue for which she is unfortunately too often distinguished, make her a formidable verbal antagonist, especially in a controversy with a member of her own sex, and if the occasion prompts it, it is probable that she can successfully support the fluent expression of her anger and resentment with very vigorous arms.

All those qualities that signify a concentration of sinister feeling are found more fully developed in the wives than in the husbands, and their manner of giving expression to these, whether in word or deed, is much more forcible and reckless of consequences, but at the same time they are more dissimulative and secretive when it is necessary to be so to attain some object which they have in view.   Their moral influence over their husbands is often pernicious ; much of the crime which the latter commit is secretly or openly instigated by the wives, who frequently go so far as to be active accomplices themselves, in gross as well as petty violations of law.   Unhappily, many are inclined, too, to stimulate their husbands to be insolent to the whites, and to rebel against the authority which employers have the right to exercise under contract.   Their bearing when thrown with members of the white race is often presumptuous, when there is no reason why it should be, apart from the spirit of antagonism which seems to have been engendered in their own hearts ; and the consequence is that the whites avoid all intercourse with them, unless domestic servants, all communication being generally held indirectly. Although shrewder and more intelligent than their husbands, yet they are, on the whole, more superstitious, and for this reason they are the principal supporters of the notorious trick doctors, their faith in the occult powers of these rank impostors being implicit. As their controversies among themselves are carried on with so much violence and bitterness, when their animosity is thoroughly aroused, they are eager to turn to whatever will ensure gratification for their vehement spite and resentment, and they are sunk low enough in credulity to believe that supernatural agencies can be compelled to intervene in their behalf.

With all her faults, and these are numerous and in some instances forbidding, the wife is generally kind in sickness. However cruel she may be ordinarily, and however indifferent to many forms of suffering, she is apt to be attentive at the bedside of extreme illness. This seems to be due more to the morbidity that colors all her thoughts of death, than to tenderness of heart ; for her solicitude is characterized by an increasing superstitiousness as the life in the dying person declines, and it reaches its climax at the end of the last scene when the body is buried. The interest which she feels in all the ghastly details is the source of pleasure to her, without any tincture of pain because they are sombre and mournful. Her sensibilities are touched in an agreeable and not in a harsh and discordant way. The

fact that it is a final parting, and therefore calculated to
lacerate her feelings, seems to enter less into her state of
mind under the circumstances than the awful mystery of
dissolution and the life beyond the grave ; and the result
is that the sickness of a comparative stranger concerns
her as much, and his death makes her as sad as if he
were a close and familiar relative or bound to her by
still stronger and more intimate ties.   Whatever is the
cause of her agitation, it has the same effect upon her
conduct as if she were actuated by unalloyed anxiety
about the condition of the patient, and by genuine sorrow, however short the time which it may last, if he
dies.

Such is the general temper of the wives.   It is they
who really mould the institution of marriage among the
plantation negroes ; to them its present degradation is
chiefly ascribable, for they are less sensible of its different obligations and more ignorant of its true objects than
their husbands even.   Until a fundamental change takes
place in their character, there can be no hope of improvement in the observance by either sex of this relation,
which is just as vital as that of parent and child.   If
there is any influence now to originate and complete this
change, it is difficult to discover it, and it seems highly
improbable that there will be any in the near future,
since the women are being further and further withdrawn
every year from the means that now exist of softening
and elevating their dispositions.

III.

MASTER AND SERVANT.

THE lavish hospitality of the planters in the age of slavery was due not only to the pleasure that they found in entertaining guests, but also to the great number of servants which that institution itself permitted ; a much larger retinue of these was attached to each residence than the ordinary tasks of the household demanded, for the cost of supporting domestics was so small that the luxury of having many, even when a few were sufficient to perform all that was required to be done, could be indulged in without any extravagance. The reception of as many guests as the capacity of each house allowed entailed, in reality, but little pecuniary outlay, as the plantation furnished an abundance of provisions, and but little trouble, as there were servants enough to see to the wants of the visitors, however numerous or exacting. The result of the war checked this spirit of hospitality at once, not only because it diminished the general prosperity of the planters, and thus compelled an abridgment of all unnecessary expenses, but also because it put the whole system of household attendance on a different footing. To have to pay the servants in money instead of merely supplying them with food, clothing, and shelter, as formerly, was a new and important addition to the domestic burdens ; in consequence the number of servants who are hired under the present régime for any length of time has been curtailed very much, but, nevertheless, the number still employed would be out of proportion to the means of the planters, if the amount of wages paid to them was not comparatively trivial. The deficiency, however, is covered by furnishing cabins and rations to them free.

The spirit of the social life of the principal planters is essentially the same as it used to be ; the old love of hospitality has not changed ; it is only gratified in a simpler way than formerly. A great store of provisions is still drawn from the resources of the plantation ; the families of the laborers still offer a latitude of choice in the selection of permanent and casual servants, who are ready to perform all the duties of the household at low rates of compensation. These show the same desire now as when they were slaves to act in this capacity, for the life they lead as such is gentler than that of the laborers, although more confining ; the tasks are lighter and easier ; the wages paid are higher, and there are many perquisites that amount to a considerable profit in the course of a year. They are not insensible, either, to the sentimental distinction of the position as compared with that of a hand in the fields or an artisan in the workshop. If the planters were to advance in prosperity, the habits of hospitality that distinguished them before the war would be fully revived, and as a result there would be as great a demand for the domestic service of the negroes as ever ; the number that would then be found in the principal residences would be as large as it once was. This is already observed in the homes of the wealthiest planters, who, in the spirit of former times, look upon a retinue of servants as the main convenience secured by fortune. As they have been accustomed to the negro from childhood, and understand his character, they prefer to employ him alone as a servant, although they are keenly aware of his deficiencies, and although the influences of freedom have worked an important change in his disposition. They dislike white domestics in comparison, for these demand a greater share of consideration, and are more exacting in their requirements. Such servants are unknown among them, both because the negroes can be engaged more cheaply, and because they have degraded household service to such an extent that not even individuals of the plainest and poorest class of native whites are willing to occupy such a position, and the white servants brought from abroad would be so isolated that they would soon become discontented and abandon their employment.

As slaves the negroes played, on the whole, a more important because a much more confidential part than they do now in the sacred associations of the family circle of their master and the principal events of his family history. Their fidelity and docility and the gentleness and indulgence with which they were generally treated, softened the aspect of that extreme power which he had of moulding their destinies according to his own interest or caprice. Their fundamental relation to him was such that they had little identity apart from his, and few memories other than those which had been impressed upon their minds in his household. All that occurred in their lives without the boundary of those familiar precincts was of far less significance to them than what happened within it. There the chief portion of the twenty-four hours of each day was spent; there they passed from youth to old age, and when they grew too infirm to perform their usual duties, they were supported until they died, but in the interval they frequently revisited the house to which they had been so long accustomed, or they themselves were visited by its inmates.

This spirit of loyal affection, which had its growth in the peculiar influences of slavery alone, animates a few of this older class, who still retain their situations in the households of the planters. Their disposition towards the latter has not changed now that they are paid monthly wages instead of receiving as formerly the mere necessaries of life for their work. Their conduct towards their masters is marked by a cheerful submission, mingled with an emotion of strong attachment that leads them to unite their fortunes with those of the white families with whom they live, as completely and unconsciously as if the tie was permanent and obligatory and not, as it is, temporary and optional. This number, however, is small, and is diminishing every year in the course of nature. The individuals who take their places are more responsive to the influences of the present age, either because they belong to the generation that has grown up since the war, or because they have broken away from the authority of that past which has already sunk into a tradition. Even where there would seem to be many local influences resembling those that prevailed in the age of slavery to draw master and servant into the same social relations that they then held to each other, there is plainly observable a great difference of spirit under the kindness of the one and the subserviency of the other. All the numerous and perplexing responsibilities of proprietorship in the body of the servant as a slave were destroyed at a stroke when that servant was emancipated. With the extinction of these responsibilities there passed away as a part of the ancient system much of that personal interest which the master had felt in the servant as an individual who was dependent on him and who must be directed in the most intimate affairs of his private life. When the negro became a citizen, the identity of his fortunes with those of his master was broken ; with the divergence of their destinies a new relation arose, which, while it was like the old in some things, was very unlike it in many things. It is now a business connection merely, formed at will, and interrupted at will on either side, and rarely elevated above this commonplace character by any ardent feeling of devotion on the part of the servant, or by unreserved confidence or warm attachment on the part of the master.

The general life of the servants in the household is necessarily the same as it was in the age of slavery. They still receive the new-born infant into their arms ; they nurse the young child with maternal fondness ; they gather in a beaming throng behind the assembly of guests at the family weddings ; at gay entertainments they look on unrebuked at the dancers in the drawing-room ; they watch through the night with patient solicitude at the bedside of the sick ; they shroud the dead for that breathless slumber which shall never be broken ; and crowd about the grave when the body is committed to the earth. But in spite of the closeness of their connection with these cheerful and mournful scenes, we discover, from the conduct of their master and his family towards them, that the reciprocity of feeling that unites them is only superficial after all. As long as the servants were slaves, for instance, there was frequent communication between their dwellings and the residence of their owner. The inmates of the latter were informed of all the incidents that joined to make up the humble history of the firesides of the cabins. They attended the different marriages of their domestics there, presented each couple with substantial bridal gifts, and furnished forth the tables for the bridal feast ; they stood and observed the throng when a party was given there, and their presence did not dash the gayety of the occasion ; they visited those who were sick and supplied them with medicines, clothing, and proper nourishment ; and if the illness ended fatally in any instance, they showed respect or affection for the dead by going to the funeral and raising a stone above the grave. In short, they testified in many ways the interest which they felt in ·the households of their servants ; and it was an interest which these looked upon as their right, but which they did not value the less for that reason. All of this has now, in great measure, passed away, in consequence of the more formal character which the relation of master and servant has assumed ; the latter neither expects nor wishes his master to be concerned about his private affairs, and the master in turn neither feels nor shows any disposition to be so. He is content to allow the social barrier which freedom has raised to stand as it is. Even if he sought to break it down, his overtures would not be met in a hearty way. If the servant or any member of his family falls sick, then the master is generally kind and helpful, but he is influenced rather by an impulse of common humanity than by personal affection. He rarely attends the weddings, entertainments, or religious meetings of his domestics. His example in this is imitated by his family ; and the result is as complete a separation between the home-life of the master and that of the servant as if there was no social tie whatever between the two.

With the decline of the master's social influence over

the servant many important changes have taken place in the character of the servant himself. As a slave he was instinctively docile and tractable, whether the master was lax in his discipline or not, for the nature of the relation was such that the domestic never lost sight for a moment of the subordination and helplessness of his position. We do not observe this now. Under the new system it depends upon the bearing of his master whether he is useful or not, for of all men who are compelled by their situation in life to earn their support in a menial capacity, and under orders, no one responds more quickly or fully than he to the spirit that animates his superior in their association. If the latter, for instance, is destitute of an executive turn, or is careless in his management, or descends to personal familiarity, then the servant is slothful, perverse, and even impertinent, for he has a very shrewd insight into moral weakness, and is too much a creature of impulse not to govern his deportment by the conclusions of his observation, whether hostile to his real interests or not. But if, on the other hand, the master is exacting and resolute, and at the same time, considerate, just, and discriminating, the servant is alert, industrious, and expeditious, unless he is peculiarly worthless by nature or has been demoralized by unusual circumstances. To bring him to the greatest usefulness it is necessary that he should be required to conform to certain fixed standards of conduct to which he will not rise of his own voluntary motion, or if he should do so, he will not adhere to them long. He rarely discharges his duties to the best of his ability, unless he is under the strictest supervision, his inclination being to allow his energies to relax as soon as the pressure that has controlled him has been removed.

When driven, so to speak, he can be confidently relied upon as a servant, if he is not exposed to too much temptation ; if the terms of commands given him are not so complex as to lead to mental confusion, into which he easily falls ; if too long a time is not to elapse before he must obey them ; or if not too much time is to be taken up in executing them, for although his ordinary disposition is to comply, yet his memory is treacherous, not retaining impressions of any kind long, even when he may wish to remember. For this reason, as well as because he is heedless and indolent naturally, the negro is generally untrustworthy as a domestic, if he is not superintended without intermission, or if his memory is not frequently refreshed ; and he will display this relaxation of effort and forgetfulness of mind whether he is acting as a superior through others, or is the immediate instrument himself. Few duties requiring intelligent, constant, and close attention are imposed upon him if the result of carelessness or thoughtlessness would be either dangerous or ruinous ; and the same may be said of him in connection with any employment that demands unusual patience, firmness, and self-possession. This inability to be watchful, prudent, and self-controlled for any length of time without alteration is displayed even when he knows that by allowing his mind to wander he is putting his life in jeopardy or injuring his material interests irretrievably. It is a trait which he seems to be incapable of either eradicating or repressing. His philosophy of life appears too often to be that the smaller the trouble and precaution taken the more easily and smoothly the world moves, and that order and precision are to be deprecated because they make necessary more or less activity, mental as well as physical. But as the spirit of docility enters more deeply into his disposition than even the spirit of indolence, he does not draw back or rebel when he is coerced. The pressure of legitimate authority brings a force to bear upon him that overcomes the strength of the fundamental qualities of his character that are running in powerful opposition. When he is under steady discipline, he cannot be extolled too highly for the readiness with which he assumes and the alacrity with which he pushes to a conclusion tasks that may be very different from the work which he is engaged to do, or foreign to his experience ; and he will show the same promptness, however late the hour of the night at which he is aroused, or however unexpected the occasion. This is to be attributed just now far more to that instinct of obedience which has been transmitted to him from his immediate forefathers, and to those lessons which have been inculcated by the meanness of his fortunes, than to the general character of his race. The traditions and influences of slavery have made the disposition of the freedmen at least more compliant and obliging than it would otherwise have been. While this submissiveness, which the negro now shows when the reins of authority over him are held with a firm hand, will decline as time progresses, his native cheerfulness and good humor will remain unaffected by his condition, whatever it may be. It is these qualities that largely influence the master of the present day to value him highly as a servant, for if he were sullen of mind as well as short of memory, and surly of aspect in addition to being frequently careless and negligent in conduct, he would be unendurable as a personal attendant. His thoughtless disposition may produce much disorder and suffer much uncleanliness around him, but its very easiness excites a lurking partiality, however exasperating its consequences occasionally. It is the disposition of an undisciplined child in its indifference to the relation of cause and effect; and like the disposition of a child, too, it prompts the master to overlook deficiencies that he would not excuse if the servant were white and not black. He goes even further than this : he does not apply to the servant the same moral standard that he applies to individuals of his own race. His inclination is rather to pity than to condemn the domestic, should the latter trespass against decorum or even honesty, experience or prejudice causing the master to believe that his servant is so undisciplined by the turn of his native qualities that he cannot properly be held responsible for his conduct ; or if he can be and should be, then the general character of his race is so defective that the person who would be employed to fill the position vacated by his summary dismissal would not be found to be less infirm in his disposition or more circumspect in his behavior. The master argues—whether justly or not—that he would merely put himself to much unnecessary inconvenience to enter into a contract with a new domestic when it is not probable that he will be better than the old, and not improbable that he will be worse.

If the servant is merely a pilferer in a small way, an effort is made to remove him from temptation ; and if his duties are such that it is impossible to do this, a close supervision is exercised over him as a temporary corrective beyond which no remedy is sought ; and this supervision has to be unremitting, in consequence of which it becomes in time very irksome. But should it be omitted on a single occasion, though the servant may have been thwarted during the course of many months, yet he will

gratify himself at the first opportunity he has of doing
so, in proportion to the length of his previous deprivation.

Occasionally the servant who is favored most highly in
the household is the one upon whom the least dependence can be put when tempted to do wrong. The general bearing of his master towards him is not affected by
a clear recognition of his weaknesses. The amiability of
the servant ; his ready and obedient spirit under firm
management ; above all, and it sounds like a strange
paradox, the innocence of his immorality, conciliate the
good-will and soften the spirit of condemnation in the
master, when the wrongful acts themselves if contem-
plated abstractly would alienate all feelings of kindness
or forgiveness. The master's confidence in the disposition of his servant is by the discovery of certain infirmities destroyed only to the extent of those infirmities ;
it does not follow at all that the latter's whole character is corrupt because it is totally unworthy of respect
in certain phases. He may be an incorrigible rogue, for
instance, and yet he will stop at no self-sacrifice to
preserve the general property, or even the life, of his master when either is in sudden danger of destruction ; he
may be indefatigable in stirring up political hatred
against the master, either directly or indirectly, and yet
will serve him with a promptness, cheerfulness, and industry that go far to soothe the feeling of distrust, which
his course has aroused. The master vents his passing
emotion of indignation and repugnance in pungent language, but he always ends by accepting his servant just
as he is with a mingled spirit of helplessness, resignation,
and philosophy, tempered by real liking and even affection. He will persist in conferring many benefits upon

that servant at the very time that he expresses his inability to esteem him, and will even impair his own interests to assist the servant, as a substantial acknowledgment of his good qualities as a domestic, however detestable his characteristics as a man. Underlying all these superficial evidences of good will, however, on the part of the master, there is found a deep distrust of the servant's character, however excellent apparently, if it should be put to a prolonged test. He places no confidence in the domestic's affection, no reliance upon his fidelity, no trust in his honesty, if circumstances should arise calculated to subject the strength of these qualities to a protracted trial ; and this premonition of the master tinctures his strictures with cynicism and breathes the spirit of contempt into his very praises.

It is remarkable how little the habits of the average negro are changed by long and intimate association as a servant with the most refined and educated white people. For instance, he has no native appreciation of order and no innate love of cleanliness and it is almost impossible even by the most persistent instruction to inculcate in him a taste for either ; on the contrary, it is not unjust to say that disorder and untidiness are positively agreeable to him and continue so. As long as he is carefully overlooked and directed, his conduct is not open to censure in this respect, for he responds to command cheerfully and obeys readily, but as soon as a rigorous superintendence is withdrawn, he shows an indifference to the condition of his surroundings that soon makes a very visible impression. The necessity of having to contend with this trait of the servant is very troublesome, and the struggle is prolonged and uninterrupted. However well-trained he may be in the performance of his household duties, or however obedient in conforming to the slightest wish of his master, he does not always show in the character of his own cabin that he has taken to heart the spirit of those admonitions to which he may listen attentively at the moment, and act upon generally while he is in the precincts of the planter's residence. No great difference in the point of comfort or neatness is observed between his home and that of the ordinary laborer, although he enjoys many perquisites out of the reach of the latter and is paid higher wages. It is true that various articles, useful as well as ornamental, are found in his dwelling that are rarely seen in the houses of the common hands, such, for instance, as pictures fly-specked and embrowned by smoke or dust, or an old-fashioned clock or rocking-chair or a worn rug or carpet, or a plate and bowl ; or there hangs in the wardrobe, perhaps, a shabby suit cut after a recent fashion, or a soiled bonnet, or a torn pair of gloves, or other finery that has passed through its best days. These have been presented by the different members of the family upon which he attends, but leaving them out of view, there are as a rule no other very conspicuous evidences that the head of the cabin passes the greater part of his life amidst the improving influences of superior refinement. His children appear in soiled and shabby clothing that could be mended and cleansed without expense ; the furniture is often allowed to remain broken when the work of a few minutes would set it in a proper condition again ; the floor to continue foul when a few sweeps of the broom would brush it clean ; the weeds to choke the vicinity of the dwelling when a dozen swathes of the scythe would cut them down. He generally erects his sty so near at hand that the air is tainted with offensive and unwholesome odors ; he frequently chooses sites for his out-houses where they will become unsightly objects ; and does many things besides to impair the healthfulness or injure the aspect of his environment which prudence or the possession of ordinary taste would have prohibited.

Even after a service of many years in the household of his employer, the principal characteristics of his race as developed in him, remain substantially as they are in individuals of his own color who have not been brought in the range of the same elevating social influences. Logically enough the constitutional differences of disposition between the master and servant as the representatives of two races, stand out in the most marked juxtaposition in their domestic connection, but contact leaves their original qualities essentially as they were. Master and servant indeed affect each other only to an insignificant degree and in unimportant things. It is remarkable that this should be so in the case of the negro, for he is the weaker, the more impressionable, and the dependent party. All the subtle power of the family life of his employer is brought to bear upon him directly, and it merely breaks through the surface of his character. He is of an imitative turn to a certain extent, and easily catches distinctions of deportment or peculiarities of dress, but on the whole, he is not responsive to that underlying and far-reaching sentiment that shapes the conduct of an upright master, near whose person his time is spent and to whose authority he submits without reserve. Such association unquestionably makes him more gentle in his bearing, but it does not deeply color his judgment in relation to his duties as a husband, a father, or a citizen ; it does not, as a rule, improve his moral tone so far as to cause him to condemn severely every form of immorality or even criminality. He is just as emotional and ignorant in his religious opinions as the most uncouth and illiterate laborer, just as superstitious in his general creed and as credulous of the supernatural. Among the negroes who have the most unshaken faith in " tricking," are house servants who have lived under conditions that seem very hostile to the entertainment of such ridiculous and puerile beliefs. However long, too, they may have been connected with their master's residence, there is no conspicuous sign of their shrinking from intimate association with the rudest persons of their race, in accordance with the promptings of acquired refinement. They share their sympathies and emotions with the field hands, and apparently no influence emanating from the positions they fill to modify their tastes and ideas, raises any social barrier of consequence between them; they intermarry with these freely and meet them in the most familiar social intercourse. But this is perhaps natural after all, for it is only in a few points that they are distinguishable from each other, these few being of no marked importance in their bearing on character, as they are superficial and not fundamental.

IV.

BLACKS AND WHITES.

THE diminished intimacy of the relation of master and servant is reflected with exaggeration in that growing social spirit which is moving the negro and white man with equal force to withdraw still further from each other. This disposition is more energetic than seems to be warranted by the mere fact that the institution of slavery has been abolished and every influence that emanated from it dissipated, or directed in the way of an early disappearance. Emancipation destroyed at one stroke the original bond of union, but the social divorce of the two races is much more marked than would have been thought possible, in the past, in the light of their local proximity and their partial dependence upon each other in an economic sense. The causes that have promoted their political opposition are soon discovered and are easily understood, but the reasons that are widening the social breach between them, are subtler and, therefore, more obscure. That the white people entertain a deep-seated social antipathy to the negro is manifest to the most careless observer; but whether this is due to the contempt and disdain which were bred in them by his former degraded condition, when his social inferiority was legalized; or whether it is to be laid at the door of his intellectual ignorance, personal uncleanliness, and moral infirmities, now that he is free; or whether it should be

attributed after all to a narrow and unthinking prejudice
that originates in a mere difference of color, is open to
discussion. The strong probability is that this state of
feeling is the result of all these powerful influences combined ; but to whatever it should be ascribed, it has had
a very vigorous and far-reaching effect in confirming an
independent tendency of the negro to live apart to himself. No one is more conscious than he of this underlying sentiment in the hearts of the white people ; he knows
very well that beneath the surface of their kindness to him,
even when it takes the form of the most open and sincere
affection, there lurks an active and resolute sensitiveness
that would rise in alarm the instant he sought, unwittingly or intentionally, to cross the social dead-line. However genial, therefore, or however friendly their demeanor
to him, he is fully aware that one forward act or ven-
turous word on his part would, at once, enkindle that
emotion of repugnance which is always smouldering in
their breasts, and which only requires the application of
the proper match to set it aflame. The social attitude of
the white people towards him is remarkable. Their conduct, capricious, irregular, and inconsistent as it seems, is
yet governed by an unwritten law, that is never changed
and never relaxed. In the midst of the most familiar intercourse, apparently, there is an unconscious mental
reservation, an instinctive assumption of superiority by
them, that gives the association a peculiar character,
which the negro, heedless and impulsive as he is, appre-
ciates by intuition. Even now, when the white people
are so much more guarded in their demeanor than they
were in the era of slavery, they often bear themselves
towards him in a way that would be an admission of social equality, but for this subtle difference of spirit. As

soon, however, as the bare idea of such equality is suggested to their minds by his manner of accepting such advances, they shrink back with unconcealed disgust and resentment, or show their indignation in a still more unmistakable way. The very fear of being misunderstood causes them to be much more circumspect in their social relations with him than they would otherwise be. All those social condescensions on their part that did so much to alleviate the hardships of slavery are, in consequence, neglected almost entirely in their present association with his race.

There can be no doubt, however, that the reluctance of the whites to enter into the general social life of the negroes is due, in some measure, to the attitude of the negroes themselves. The former rarely attend now the social celebrations of the blacks, not only because they shrink from such intimate contact, but also because their presence arouses a spirit of uneasiness and discomfort in the colored participants, who desire to follow out their own impulses, however extravagant, unobserved by persons who, they know instinctively, would be critical, amused, or shocked. So far, therefore, as their more conspicuous social occasions are concerned, they are left to do honor to them after the manner they prefer. The nature of these occasions would be changed, and the spirit which they would exhibit dissipated, if white persons were to venture to take part in them. If, for instance, a white man, whether a clergyman by profession or a respectable citizen, who felt a lively interest in the moral welfare of his negro neighbors, were to seek to substitute himself permanently for their local preacher, and to deliver sermons in his stead every Sunday, the probability is that he would not be able to gather together a congregation, since its possible members would feel compelled, while sitting under him, to behave with self-restraint, which would mean the repression of that frantic religious excitement into which they fall so easily, and which they enjoy so much. This being the accompanying condition of his ministration, it would breathe a chill upon the enthusiasm of the negroes who might attend, and it would not be long before they would absent themselves altogether rather than forego, when they did meet devotionally, the ability to act just as the spirit of their religion moved them.

If the leading white citizens were to inform the laborers of a neighborhood of their intention to be present at one of those plantation entertainments which are occasionally given at the end of autumn, when the different crops have been harvested and stored away securely, the announcement would not be received by the negroes as a proof of friendly interest, but would be looked upon as throwing a cloud on the jollity of the future event ; and they would feel thus, not so much because the attendance of the citizens, as persons occupying the most prominent position in the community, would embarrass and disturb them, but principally because these are white men, and as such, therefore, not in sympathy with the manner in which they would abandon themselves to the intoxication of the hour. This sensitiveness on the part of the negroes is still more conspicuously displayed at the funerals, on which occasions, it would be thought, the mere solemnity of the ceremony, as well as the mournful spectacle of mortality, would stifle this emotion by making them unconscious of every thing beside. But it does not. The burial is as distinct a custom of the blacks as the religious assembly, and as vividly reflective

of their social peculiarities.   They are opposed, therefore,
to the introduction of any influence or any innovation
that would be apt to hamper them in celebrating it just
as they wished.   The white people are so well aware of
this that they are rarely prompted to go to such funerals,
however excellent a reason they may have for being
grateful to the dead, or however desirous of showing
respect to their memories.

This divergence between the social life of the one race
and that of the other in those scenes where it would be
supposed a common humanity and similar material interests would bring the members of both together, leaves a
strong impression upon the observer.   Omit the domestic
servants from consideration, who constitute only a few in
the general multitude, and it is found that the sphere in
which the negroes move socially is as wide apart from
that in which the social existence of the whites is passed,
as if the two races inhabited different countries, and
were, therefore, locally cut off from each other.   Individuals representing both are constantly thrown with
each other, it is true ; negroes and white men meet as
employers and employés, or as common laborers ; but
their association stops there, and it is of a formal character as far as it goes.   The two distinct societies do not
join, when they come together at all, in such a way as to
result in a complete blending, however brief, of their
separate systems.   The remotest anticipation of such
union, without reserve, even in the most insignificant and
superficial social affairs, touches the sensibilities of the
white people with as lively repugnance and abhorrence
as if it signified a descent into an unmeasurable depth of
degradation.   To acknowledge social equality in small
things is to give up the general principle which is appli-

cable equally to small and great ; and to do so in either
is to relinquish their grasp upon every thing that they
value and every thing that they love. It is to strike a
blow at the integrity of their social life ; it is to revo-
lutionize their natures, and to enfeeble their appreciation of existence itself. Until all the traditions
and emotions which their superiority of mental and
moral character, and differences of race and condition,
have created have been destroyed, they will continue
to feel as they do now. Until then, even to discuss the
probability of a change of sentiment, will be accounted as
an insult ; to justify such a change will be considered as
heinous as defending incest and rape ; and to predict it
with confidence, will be taken as a proof that the speaker,
if white, is an enemy of his people, who should, therefore, be condemned and avoided. The present strength
of this sentiment in the breasts of the white people, is
largely ascribable, and upon the most reasonable and
natural grounds, to the ignorance and licentiousness of
the typical negro of the present age that would make
him highly objectionable to refined sensibilities and cultivated minds, even if his skin were that of a Caucasian.
Intellectual blindness, moral obtuseness, and a thoughtless indulgence of every appetite have never been judged
to be lovely and attractive traits in social intercourse.
If the negro were modest and unobtrusive in his deportment, upright and honorable in his conduct, sober and
self-respecting in his disposition, intelligent and elevated
in mind, he would receive without stint that personal
respect to which his demeanor and character would
entitle him. In short, if he were in full possession of all
the noble qualities that adorn human nature, the white
people would be as little prompted to pass him by

with indifference and contempt, socially, as if he belonged to their own race, and was distinguished as a
member of it, for the same moral and mental excellence.
It is true that they would not admit him to all the privileges of their firesides, but they would cheerfully allow
him every social right to which he could properly lay
claim. So far from imitating such an ideal example
as this, the negroes frequently disclose in their intercourse with white people, an eagerness to attain to social
equality for the time being, without having any just
ground in themselves for such pretension. When thrown
with the older children of their employers, they are
pointed in addressing them by their Christian names
more often than occasion calls for, and this disposition
to gratify their desire for social recognition by an offi-
cious and presumptuous bearing, is only repressed in its
most insolent manifestations, under other circumstances,
by the resolute resentment of it on the part of its victims. In a capricious, unsteady, and impulsive way, no
man is more aspiring than the negro, and if this trait
were supported by a proportionate vigor of character
and tenacity of purpose, he would soon thrust himself,
in spite of the firmest opposition, into the greatest prominence as an individual, but he is incapable of stern and
indefatigable persistence. Admit him in his present
state of development to that social position which he
seems to value so much, and the mere consciousness of
having attained an end which he had desired so keenly,
instead of strengthening him for a further advance,
would probably turn his head beyond recovery. He
would become extremely giddy and vain, and would be
inflated with a pompous sense of his own social consequence. The inclination of the negro, when he is puffed

up in his self-love by any kind of success, however trivial, is to pass the bounds of propriety and even decency ; on the other hand, when discouraged, as he is by the smallest obstacle, he is apt to sink to the lowest point of servility. This tendency is very plainly illustrated in his association with white people. Thus the employé who is humblest and most deprecating, under exacting authority, is often one of the first to bear himself rudely and impertinently towards white persons when he can do so safely ; and in this he is influenced not so much by sinister feeling as by a childish rashness that unsettles his brain like the penetrating fumes of strong liquor. Few members of his race have that element of self-respect in their characters that would lead them to be true to an elevated conception of their own individuality, however tested, and which would move them to show anger and hatred, when under the influence of those passions, in a bold and manly way. They too frequently display the greatest cruelty when they can inflict injury, and an equal abjectness when they are overawed by force.

The white people are clearly aware of this aspiring and aggressive disposition of the negroes in a personal way, and that spirit of antagonism which it nourishes in their breasts has brought about a complete separation between the two under many circumstances where there was the most familiar contact formerly. Two notable instances of this may be referred to. Thus, before the slaves were set free, the white and black children mingled at all hours of the day in a common enjoyment of the various sports and amusements of their age, whether pursued in the house or in the field ; and this constant companionship gave birth to a kindness and affection for each other that were often deep and lasting.   Such inter-course between the children of the two races is rarely observed now, because the white people are, as a rule, strict in forbidding theirs to turn to such society for diversion.   They are induced to do this, primarily, by antipathy of race that makes them careful to preserve the barriers between the negroes and themselves in their present strength and firmness, which, they believe, can only be done by keeping the two races as far apart socially as possible.   The children can only associate together, now, on a footing of equality ; the relation which they formerly bore to each other, even in comparative in-fancy, can no longer be maintained.   An admitted superi-ority on one side and an accepted inferiority on the other, as soon as their intelligence could recognize that there was a distinction, was not only a necessary characteristic but also the real basis of that relation under the old sys-tem.   But this is not so now that the emancipation of the slave has brought about so many social changes.   That difference in the nature of the terms of association on which the children of the two races would now meet, would seem to be unimportant in the light of their youth, but such equal association, however completely it may terminate as time advances, jars upon the sensitive pre-judices of the white people and makes them anxious to forbid it altogether.   A subordinate, but powerful con-sideration, too, is their very reasonable objection to the moral effect of such companionship, for the young ne-groes unfortunately are so ignorant of those lessons that enforce propriety of speech and deportment that it is not surprising that prudent and watchful parents should not regard them as fit associates for their offspring, espe-cially when the latter are still at an impressionable age.

It is not to be supposed that they would overlook in such children what they would undoubtedly censure severely if those children were not black, but white, who set an equally unhappy example and exerted an influence as dangerous. Even before emancipation, such companionship, hedged in as it was then by so many restrictions, was not beneficial morally, but was unavoidable, owing to the relation that bound the slave to the master.

A far more remarkable evidence of the social antipathy of the white people to the negro is the fact that illicit sexual commerce between the two races has diminished so far as to have almost ceased, outside the cities and towns, where the association being more casual, is more frequent. This is due to the attitude of the whites, for the negresses are less modest as a class at the present day than they were before the abolition of slavery, since they are now under no restriction at all. In consequence of this reserve on the part of white men, the mulattoes are rapidly decreasing in numbers with the progress of time, and the negroes as a mass are gradually but surely reverting to the original African type. Before many decades elapse, this influence, working in the domestic life of the race, must impress itself profoundly upon the moral and intellectual disposition of its members, and thus shape and govern their social and political destinies; but its force will be most direct and powerful in its social bearing, for the only possibility of the social amalgamation of the two peoples must turn upon the half-breed as the primary medium of transfusion. As his skin darkens in its return to the tint which distinguished that of his remote ancestors, the prospects of blacks and whites lawfully mixing their blood fades to the thinnest shadow of probability. There was little improper intercourse between

mere physical luxuries which it is able to purchase, but rather as a surviving exponent of that power by which he was coerced during the period of his slavery. He honors the strength of a vigorous frame only as long as he is in danger of being soundly cudgelled, but for those high qualities of mind and spirit that constitute the essential and fundamental differences between man and man, such as justness, probity, dignity, and purity, he has no esteem, unless they are supported by fortune. As the lowest class of the white people have no riches to impress his imagination, and as he does not value difference of character, he is disposed to hold them in lively contempt, and very often is only prevented from giving expression to his scorn in rude language, by his fear of corporal retaliation at their hands. They are well aware of this impulse, and as they return it with an acrimony keener in proportion to their greater capacity for steady and intense feeling, the social antagonism between the two is ardent and uncompromising. Now, this class of the white people have always been very much under the personal influence of those of their race who enjoy the highest social prominence, among whom, the hostility to social equality with the negro is tinctured with the contempt of a caste that is founded not only upon refinement, education, and wealth, but also upon distinctions of race. As long as they continue to exercise the same influence upon the classes below them, the association of the latter with the negro in a social way, will retain its present bent of unconcealed aversion, even though time dissipates many of those prejudices of race that now divide them. There is no evidence that this influence has diminished in consequence of the pecuniary disasters entailed upon

the highest rank of citizens by the failure of the
Southern cause in the late war, and in no direction has
it been exerted with more earnestness than towards
sustaining that social repugnance which keeps the lowest
class aloof from the negroes, and which alone obstructs
their social union.

This feeling on the part of the leading white people is
not inconsistent with kindness and good-will to the
negro. They like the individual because he is generally
amiable and obliging. Then, too, he is associated with
all the principal scenes in the course of their lives,
and is thus invested with that personal interest which
is created by intimate and uninterrupted intercourse.
As long as his bearing is unobtrusive and self-respecting,
he cannot complain of their manner of receiving
him, or the character of their disposition towards him.
On the other hand, they never vary in disliking and
condemning his race not only on account of its improvidence, unreliability, and moral deficiencies, but
also because its mere presence in their midst is a direct
menace to the tranquillity of their social life, the stability of their political institutions, and the prosperity of
their material affairs. The freedman has, on the whole,
proved himself to be a faithful laborer under supervision,
but his children, born and educated under the influences
of the new system, are not so amenable to authority
and are much less inclined to work. This has increased
those industrial obstacles which the white people are
anxious to surmount, and their sentiment towards the
race has been less favorable in proportion. Futher-
more, they entertain the belief that the low standard
of living which distinguishes the negroes as a mass,
renders it impossible for any class of immigrant laborers

to compete with them, which has resulted in a serious injury to the sections of the State where the blacks predominate, inasmuch as families who would have removed thither, have been discouraged from doing so. The great political power of such a horde of ignorant voters is still more calculated to disturb the equanimity of the white people, and inspire them with a fear that is inconsistent with any confidence in the negroes as a body ; who constitute such an instrument for evil in the hands of ingenious, selfish, and worthless adventurers, that the constant danger of their being turned to such unscrupulous account has hitherto invested their political existence with a sinister significance that has had the natural effect of repelling their former owners, who alone are likely to suffer any injury by it.

Beneath all this antipathy of the whites to the negroes as a race, we detect a clear recognition of the wisdom of accepting their presence in the community, in that utilitarian spirit which will strive to turn it to advantage, by improving their intellectual and moral condition, as far as it is possible to do so, as a preparation for a sober and honorable career in the future. The white people argue that the blacks are among them apparently to remain, and unless they can be made useful to society, they will probably jeopardize its existence, and undoubtedly destroy its prosperity ; all proper means should, therefore, be employed to convert them into energetic and conservative citizens. With that view, the members of the dominant class have supported the public-school system with a liberality that is barely justified by their private means, as it seems to be the only feasible agency by which the desired object can be accomplished, owing to the social separation and antagonism between the two races.

It is difficult to detect the exact character of the general opinion which the negro entertains of his white neighbors. It is obvious, however, that the authority which the white people once exercised over him from the mere fact that they were white, is fast declining, which shows that his respect for a white skin has diminished. He is still easily repressed by any show of force by white men, because he knows them to be determined and courageous, while he is conscious of his own timidity ; but that undefined notion which he formerly had of the superiority of the other race, and which he still has to a considerable degree even now, is no longer powerful in controlling his conduct by checking his natural impulsiveness. There is at present no purely sentimental influence to overawe him in his general relations with that race, even under circumstances where formerly he would have shrunk back in humility or terror ; and it is this state of mind towards the great mass of the whites, which arises out of thoughtlessness rather than deliberation, that makes it of the gravest importance that all which has a tendency to inflame the social antagonism of the two peoples should be earnestly deprecated. As the negro drifts, with the passage of time, further away from the white man, this aggressive social independence will be offensively manifested very frequently, and if he were as firm and intrepid as he is irresolute and timorous, its consequences would be fatal to the tranquillity of any community of which he formed a part. Very unfortunate is the situation of that community in which there are such distinct and vigorous social forces as these represented by the two races, respectively moving forward in the same direction, but conflicting quite often enough to create and diffuse a general feeling of uneasiness and disquietude. And this occasional friction cannot be ignored, however eager the inclination to do so, so obvious and so pernicious is the impression which it leaves upon the general destinies of the common country.

V.

THE NEGRO AND THE COMMONWEALTH.

THE presence of the negro even as a slave put the safety of every community in which he lived in jeopardy, but that presence at once assumed a far more alarming significance when the fetters were suddenly struck from his limbs and all the rights of citizenship were conferred upon him. To endow him with privileges so important in themselves, and so momentous in their possible consequences, was only justifiable as a measure that was necessary for the protection of the liberty of the beneficiary. As to whether it was really necessary or not, it would now be idle to discuss. There can be no difference of opinion, however, as to the total insufficiency of the preparation which he had received for exercise of responsibilities so grave and far-reaching as those that are incident to suffrage. Illiterate, credulous, feeble in judgment, weak in discrimination, a child in his habits of dependence and self-indulgence, accessible to every temptation and with little ability to resist, without a hope or aspiration above his physical pleasures, he was raised on the instant from the level of a beast of burden to the full enjoyment of the noblest prerogative of freedom— the right to vote. It was virtually the admission to the franchise of a man who, from the degradation of his previous condition, was as incapable as a savage out of the bush of understanding the duties of that new situation in which the force of circumstances, which he had neither directed nor anticipated, had placed him. The moral and mental disposition of each individual, as well as the great numerical strength of his race, might have been expected with absolute confidence to invest its members as a body with such a sinister political power as had never been paralleled before. To confer the right of suffrage upon them, even for the purpose of educating and sobering them, was an experiment that was certain to inflict the most serious injury on every social and political institution before the process of instruction and improvement could be finished satisfactorily. Consummated in the period of indescribable anarchy and bewilderment that succeeded the close of the war, its inevitable tendency was to prolong, if not to perpetuate, the state of general confusion that then prevailed. Under its operation it seemed to be impossible that any thing that remained of the social and political polity that had been valued and revered in the past could survive even for a decade or generation, and it would not have done so but for the impotence of the negro and the firmness of the Anglo-Saxon. The momentousness of the issue raised rather than lowered the courage of the whites, and the stress of that struggle to retain what was very dear to them as men and citizens, which followed, touched the sensibilities and strengthened the resolution of the lowest and highest among them alike, consolidating them by the influence of a common sympathy, and stimulating them by the force of a common motive. In casting their ballots the political principle sank out of sight in the supreme importance of the social principle to be sustained ; in short, it was a social rather than a political question that was to be decided on the occasion of every election. The ballot was in reality an instrument of self-defense, according to his particular view, in the hands of the white man ; he deposited his vote for the purpose of preserving his social life as unchanged as possible, and to accomplish this it was essential that he should maintain his political ascendency. His triumph at the polls secured further the dignity and stability of public affairs, a general respect for law and order, economy of administration, and fairness of taxation ; all these things bore directly upon his material interests and appealed to his selfishness as keenly as the preservation of his social institutions in their original integrity appealed to his sentiment.

On the other hand, the negro, too, looked upon the ballot as his most effective weapon of self-defense. If the right of suffrage was bestowed upon him for that reason, then he accepted it emphatically in a responsive spirit ; he clung to it with a tenacity and anxiety that were only explicable in the light of his dense ignorance and extreme credulity, which placed him under the dominion of white leaders, who made use of both, at the expense of truth and honor, to promote their own selfish designs. These fostered, in every way, those groundless apprehensions as to the security of his newly acquired rights that lurked in his heart after he was set free ; and by the force of their ingenious and unscrupulous representations, he came to regard the ballot-box as the only barrier between him and his virtual re-enslavement. They obtained such an influence over him by crafty and unconscionable appeals to his fears, that they inspired him with but one political principle, namely, to vote always in opposition to the whites. That was his permanent policy, and he followed it out with a wonderful singleness of purpose.

No just and accurate insight into his real political disposition in the past can be gotten unless this fact is taken
into consideration, for, up to a certain date, it was the
principal motive of his political conduct, being more
powerful even than natural antipathy of race.   Very unfortunately, however, in using the ballot as a means of
self-protection, he unconsciously employed it as a powerful instrument of attack ; and the consequence has been
that he has shown himself to be a most dangerous enemy
to stable and conservative government.   His influence
upon that political life into which he was introduced so
unexpectedly, and which he was not at all prepared to
enter, has been demoralizing in all its bearings.   To endow with citizenship an individual as ignorant and debased as he necessarily was, on account of his previous
condition of servitude, was to lower the dignity of the
suffrage to a level where it could only be regarded with
mingled contempt and alarm.   It was besmirching the
character of the highest privilege of enlightened freedom.
In making, as it did, the issues of the ballot-box as important and almost as desperate as those of the battle-
field, it was subjecting the franchise to a strain that it
could not bear without debauching, in some measure, the
spirit of political methods, and, thereby, the general tone
of the community.   In the contest for the preservation
of certain vital social and political principles, a subtle
callousness and insensibility were spread abroad like an
insidious and corrupting contagion.

Though the cause of this disturbance and the fountain-
head of these pernicious influences, it is hard to condemn
the negro, except for lack of political judgment and sagacity.   Owing to his unscrupulous advisers, he considered himself to be contending at the polling booth for a

principle more fundamental even than that which his former master was seeking to maintain,—a principle that involved the various rights of freedom, if not freedom itself, and if to secure that principle the community itself had to be destroyed and every institution that raised it above barbarism completely extinguished, it would not have been unnatural for him to hail the catastrophe with satisfaction, if it prevented him from being relegated to his former condition. Happily, circumstances have arisen which have done much to prove to the negro that his rights are not at all endangered by the triumph in a national election of that party which he had been taught was ready to deprive him of all his privileges of citizenship, if not remand him to the servile position which he once occupied. There had been observed for many years prior to 1884 some inclination on his part to vote with the white people when petty local offices were to be filled, an evidence that he was learning to discriminate between elections that were and those that were not vital in their relation to what he deemed to be the danger of his position. It is a proof also that he was not animated altogether by hostility to the whites in his determination to cast his ballot in opposition to them whenever the issues of the contest were of the broadest significance, as, for instance, in presidential, gubernatorial, and legislative elections ; there was a well-defined principle in his conduct, upon which he acted with not the less steadiness because it was founded upon an erroneous idea. A considerable change of sentiment was produced even among the most ignorant members of his race by the event of the national election of 1884. They observed that no curtailment of their personal rights resulted from that event in conformity with the prediction of their designing leaders; they were not only not re-enslaved, but no restriction whatever was put upon their freedom of movement ; they were as much at liberty as they ever were to form their own plans and to follow out the dictates of their own judgment and caprices.   This was a revelation of much importance to them; and it has not been without effect on subsequent elections, even when issues were involved in these that would have influenced the negroes formerly to adhere most strictly to the color line.   It is true that even in these elections the great majority have continued to vote for the candidates of their original party,[1] but many have done so by the mere force of a habit growing out of long affiliation with it ; a sufficient number cast their ballots in sympathy with the opposite party to disclose that their ranks were not wholly intact.   There is some disposition on their part now not to vote at all.   A political apathy, born of an assured sense of security, has fallen upon many of the race, and it is extending to a wider circle.   A spirit of indifference has sprung up that appears to be contagious ; now that their anxiety has been allayed, they value the right of suffrage less than they formerly did.   Gratitude is a quality that enters very little into their character, and therefore they are not led to support persistently and actively the party that set them free, simply because it emancipated them from slavery.   Few impressions linger long enough in their minds to govern their conduct, and a recollection of benefits that have been conferred upon them is not to be included in the number.   They voted with that party, not because it loosed their bonds, but because they believed that their rights were only preserved by its

[1] The Republican party.

watchfulness and constant intervention. As soon as circumstances banished this delusion, then that adhesive principle which had united them to that party began at once to relax, because no emotion as lively as fear was left to sustain it in the same vigor, and none is likely to be called into existence hereafter that will have the power to do so. A new and rapidly growing danger has arisen in consequence of this increasing latitude of political feeling and action among them. It would be impossible to find in any country so many voters whose partisanry conforms with more immediate sympathy to the seductions of bribery, as among the negroes under the pressure of that change of sentiment which is observed in them now ; and this venality is not confined to the rank and file, who can be bought up for a mere song, but it has corrupted even the most alert and intelligent leaders of their own color, who, instead of setting their fellows a good example, are most forward in receiving the price that is offered for their influence.

There can be no ground for doubt that if the negroes had consulted their true interests they would have voted in accord with the white people from the day that the right of suffrage was conferred on them, since all that served to antagonize the two races reacted very much to the injury of the weaker, and retarded its progress. As a great body of land-owners, and as the chief dispensers of employment, the white citizens were in a situation to benefit and assist their former slaves ; but as the latter elected to combine with an unscrupulous and unpatriotic white faction, and to cast their ballots inimically to the permanent welfare of the community, it is not surprising that some acrimony of feeling was engendered among those who suffered most in consequence, or that there should have been some disinclination on their part to aid men who used the power they possessed so mischievously. The substantial kindness of the whites to the individual negro, even from the close of the war, however, is illustrated by the fact that the latter, when in trouble, has always turned to them as constituting his best friends after all,—a correct and just view, for the white people have been disposed, on the whole, to excuse even his most turbulent conduct as the result of ignorance. He may be such a partisan as to assault persons of his own color for voting for his employer, and yet before the sun has set on the day of election, he will perhaps ask an important favor of that employer, and feel, if his request is complied with, that it is only what he has a right to expect. If he were to repress that unreasoning and factious spirit of political opposition which he has displayed at the very moment that he has shown his confidence in the personal kindness of the whites, then the latter would be much more inclined than they are now to help him in every way. The numerical strength of the blacks has always been a source of much anxiety to their former masters, because it put so much that vitally concerned them in jeopardy. If this fear were to be entirely removed by the action of the blacks themselves, one of the most powerful influences that perpetuates the antipathy of the white people to that race would be destroyed, leaving the most ample room for the play of generous emotions. The material interests of the two races are so identical, that any exasperating cause of disagreement between them can only terminate detrimentally to the prosperity of the community in which both dwell. Division upon the color line merely renders the antagonism already existing more intense, and to inflame that antagonism periodically is to create a tendency to disorder and decay. It is not as if two parties, separated by a divergence of opinion as to the propriety of ordinary principles, were set over against each other ; the principles here go down to the root of all the personal relations of daily life, and their continual agitation is certain to excite the most embittered prejudice and hatred in those who adhere to either side. If this agitation were to cease, and all forms of bribery were repressed, citizens of both races would, under the pressure of a common impulse, move forward together to vote for the same candidate and the same measures. An emotion of gratitude would be aroused in the hearts of the white people in consequence of the dissipation of that solicitude which they had naturally felt with respect to the stability of their public affairs. It would then be their instinctive inclination as well as their selfish interest to foster the confidence of their allies, the surest way to which would be to confer many personal kindnesses upon them, and to extend to them every opportunity of material advancement. With their attention diverted from politics, the negroes themselves would probably direct their energies more strenuously to the improvement of their general condition ; and in any event, would become a much less dangerous element in society.

The political reconciliation of the races would lead to a more cheerful and willing spirit among the white citizens in allowing the negro that share of civil rewards to which he has a legal right to aspire. As long as the latter stands apart in a distinct political organization of his own, the white voters will be as little disposed to honor him as they are to honor any political opponent. But they have even now no desire to deprive him of the right to hold such public positions as he is competent to fill without injury to the general prosperity. They are, however, warmly opposed to elevating him to offices, the duties of which require for their proper performance the exercise of knowledge, discretion, and firmness, for it is in these qualities that the negro is peculiarly deficient. Such offices, for instance, are those of supervisors, who have the administration of the county finances ; of treasurers, who have the custody of the county funds ; of assessors, who estimate the value of personal and real property ; and of justices of the peace, who are the local conservators of the law. These demand not only special fitness in the point of capacity, but also fidelity and honesty of character, and are of more local importance than the charge of a delegate to the State Legislature even. There would be a much more decided inclination among the whites to overlook even the infirmities of the negro, in distributing political rewards, if he were to lay them under a heavy obligation for party services. They are electing him now to subordinate positions in which he is exposed to no temptation, or his ignorance can do little harm : and if he proves himself competent and trustworthy, he will undoubtedly be advanced to positions of considerable dignity and responsibility. This already occurs sometimes in instances where he will be only one of a large committee, the other members being left to put such check upon his conduct as may be necessary. At present he is without political experience, without moral or intellectual strength, and without that property stake in the community that would make him careful and conservative. Even as it is, the mere force of race prejudice, however violently it might influence the dominant class, could not keep him down in the obscurity of private life, if he had sufficient ability to rise.

The negroes have produced no leaders of uncommon ability among themselves ; indeed, no individual of their race has appeared who has shown any talent for organization, or any capacity for grasping the most enlightened ideas of policy, or. disinterestedness enough to be inspired by the highest motives of patriotism. The typical black politician has been as destructive in his ambitions, and as unscrupulous in his methods, as the worst of his white associates, and far more venal. As a public speaker, he has developed great power of verbal expression, which very frequently rises to a phenomenal verbosity. If he is ever at a loss for one word, he quickly substitutes for it the first that enters his mind, whether it is apt or not ; the longer it is, and the more difficult to pronounce, the more appropriate it seems to himself and his audience. As a rule, his harangues are without any relevancy or coherence ; mere sound without sense and violence without force ; strange imitations of the model which he is aiming to copy ; a gross travesty, indeed, that would be ludicrous but for the number of voters whom the speaker represents. We find occasionally among his fellow orators one who uses very perspicuous language, not always grammatical, it is true, but not faulty enough to weaken the strength of a fairly logical argument. There is a sophomoric ring to most of their speeches, however correct, that discloses the imaginative turn or the childish immaturity of their faculties. They never lose their self-possession on the rostrum, however awkward the situation apparently ; all interruptions, though hostile and calculated to confuse being received with entire serenity of mind and blandness of demeanor. During the course of an active canvass, they deliver many speeches on the Court green at every meeting of the County Court, but they are seen in their proudest rôle in the local conventions, that meet to nominate candidates. The negro shows here a very amusing respect for parliamentary terms and usages, since he is to the extent of his knowledge an uncompromising stickler for parliamentary etiquette in its different forms. Nowhere else is that curious pomposity of manner and language, which he falls into at once, when struck with a sense of his own importance, so fully displayed. His imitative turn becomes most conspicuous under the extreme dignity and solemnity of his deportment, because these are lacking in the essential element of simplicity. As members of political committees although they may nominally occupy the leading position, the blacks, as a rule, appear to great disadvantage, for they have no executive ability, which is a logical result of the fact that they are without power of concentrated thought and attention, and are indifferent to the means, however eager to reach the end. Those who have obtained seats in the Legislature, have won no special reputation for practical capacity by an intelligent devotion to business ; and as they are generally silent members, or wandering and irrelevant when they have risen to their feet, they have exercised no marked influence on the enactment of laws, except by the votes they cast. Indeed, the majority have not been at all superior to the mass of their race in force of character or intellect ; many, in fact, have been inferior, and their election to a position of so much re_ sponsibility can only be explained on the ground of accident. The prominence of the office they occupy only brings out into the broadest contrast their incompetence to represent the interests of their own people, much less advance the general prosperity of a commonwealth.

The preachers of the negroes are their most active

politicians, as a rule, but even when they are not they
have much political influence, for they constitute, indi-
vidually, the natural leaders of their race, being elevated
to their clerical position not because they are men of
greater holiness of life or eloquence of tongue than the
rest of their fellows, but because they have more energy
and decision of character. Each one brings these qualities to bear on all occasions of public agitation from that
conspicuous coigne of vantage, his pulpit, which thus
becomes a rostrum, the religious doctrines enunciated
from thence, taking the color of his political principles,
just as, on the other hand, his political harangues have a
religious echo. The two parts of minister and orator are
played so skilfully at one and the same time that it is
impossible to distinguish them ; and the affairs of the
Hereafter and a contemporary political canvass are
mixed in inextricable confusion. His church is thus
converted into a political organization that is consoli-
dated by the religious fervor that pervades it, and pro-
pelled towards a single political end by a religious
enthusiasm that expects to be rewarded spiritually for
the performance of partisan duties. The preacher playing alternately upon the political passions and religious
fears of his congregation, or upon both at once, excites
an emotional responsiveness that is prepared to obey his
slightest injunctions ; and he does not hesitate to turn
this exalted state of feeling to the most useful account.

The political mass-meeting of the negroes is held after
nightfall, for it is only at that late hour that the laborers
can attend. The spot selected is illuminated by the
glare of torches ; and what with the waving lights, the
darkness of the background of forest, the gleaming of
the foliage overhead, the dimly outlined forms of men

huddled together, the strident voices of the speakers, and the low murmurs of assent rising from their auditors, the scene is strangely picturesque in its physical aspects and impressive in its political suggestions. It is a strong proof of the timidity of the negroes that they have not often been impelled by these occasions, the influences of which are always violent and incendiary, to inflict the grossest injury upon the white people, but excepting a certain moroseness and sullenness of demeanor, their employers observe no evidence even on the following day of the emotions of anger and hatred that had inflamed their minds so recently.

Through such men and means as these, supplemented by the white leaders, to whom reference has already been made, the negroes have obtained the whole of their political knowledge ; and that knowledge, if such scanty and defective information as they have, with respect to political principles, can be spoken of properly as knowledge at all, has been distorted by the medium through which it has been transmitted. Few are even aware that there is such an institution as the press. That powerful engine for shaping public opinion does not reach them at all ; it does not even reflect such political opinions as they may entertain. Its force of reason and passion is lost on the black voters who toil in the fields or loll about the stores ; to whom the newspaper is only a species of material in which the groceries they purchase at the stores are wrapt for security and protection. The great mass of these voters are dumb until the day of election. While the political fervor of the whites is breaking forth in so many audible and visible ways, from the hustings, in processions, and through the party organs, expressing itself from dawn until midnight in the

thousand reverberating sounds that roll from hill to hill
and valley to valley, the comparative silence and secre-
tiveness of the political sentiment of the negroes inspire
both awe and fear, so ominous do they seem, and so indicative of a strength that is to be dreaded all the more
because it is wholly numerical. Messengers, with the
proper instructions, have flitted from settlement to settlement, as if they were passing the watchword to an army
of soldiers off duty, with the injunction that it shall be
preserved from disclosure until the hour for action
arrives. And when the polls are thrown open the
colored voters run together by a common impulse from
field and forest, and cast their ballots with the regularity
and precision of a military organization. It is too much,
perhaps, to expect that men so recently emancipated,
and as credulous and illiterate as they are, would show
on such an occasion the influence of the most enlightened
principles. Studying their political spirit as then displayed, and without considering the alleviating circumstances, it is palpable that they do not ; such an expression as the public good, the commonwealth, is without
force of meaning to their minds. A people who lack, as
they do, the pride of race are incapable of the most disinterested emotions of patriotism ; a people as heedless,
thoughtless, and restless as they are can never exalt the
interests of the community above their own. They seem
to have some local attachment, but the fireside, the home,
the family are not invested in their minds with the profound meaning which is the secret of that love which all
the nationalities of mankind feel for their respective
lands, and without which this love of country cannot
exist in its highest perfection ; the consequence is that
the negroes entertain no sentimental devotion whatever

for their native soil.   Education, to the extent to which
it has been carried, has not cultivated or even produced
this spirit of patriotism by expanding the range of their
thoughts and feelings ; instead of broadening their ideas,
it appears to have only increased their egotism and their
contempt for their race.   So far they have made no real
progress in identifying themselves in a temperate way
with the duties and privileges of citizenship.   Those
who have sought to play a political part of prominence
have resembled only overgrown children making a pretense at statesmanship, while the great majority have
acted blindly upon the impulses of hatred and fear or, at
best, of personal gain.   All classes of the race are much
less in accord with the true spirit of our government
than foreigners from despotic countries who have been
naturalized.   There is no true affinity between them and
the institutions under which they live ; and whether they
will ever grow into harmony with these institutions, is a
question upon which the future alone can throw any de-
cisive light.

VI.

THE NEGRO AND THE CRIMINAL LAW.

WHEN we observe the negroes as a mass, we find that they violate the principal clauses of the Criminal Code less often than we would be led to expect at first ; but it is not a ground of surprise when we have obtained an insight into the general character of the individuals of the race. It is true that they are very impulsive, this being perhaps the most prominent trait of their disposition ; but they rarely become desperate and turbulent by the force of the most vehement passion, except when under the dominion of an ardent physical appetite. One of the most remarkable of their peculiarities is, that they have little capacity for receiving a profound impression, although the circumstances surrounding them may seem to be such as to create it inevitably. If such an impression is ever made, it is soon obliterated. Their ideas change as rapidly and unaccountably as their emotions. They do not continue long enough in one state of mind, however intense at the moment, for it to color their behavior for any length of time. Unless, therefore, they act at once when under the influence of the passing anger which sometimes sways them so violently when they happen to have cause for the warmest resentment, they are not apt to act at all, so quickly is their exasperation of feeling dissipated ; but while it lasts, they do not shrink from perpetrating any crime, however heinous, or however easily detected. It is in this humor and under such pressure as this, that nearly all the gross violations of law that are brought home to them are committed. Their power of mental concentration is not sufficient to ensure the steadiness and constancy that are necessary to the success of a malicious purpose that has to be executed with deliberation ; in other words, they lack the ability to carry out a criminal design with skill and foresight, simply because they are wanting in the qualities of subtlety, prudence and steadfastness. Oddly as it may sound, the absence of a resolute and scheming vindictiveness in the character of the negro is one of the most convincing indications of his moral feebleness, since that absence, in his instance, is not due to generosity and magnanimity, but to fickleness and instability. It should not be forgotten, too, that his usual temper is mild and easy, reflecting in its brightness and cheerfulness the sunny climate of his primitive continent. The courage of his race, if that race had been great, would have sunk into a sinister moodiness beneath the burden of sorrow and humiliation that weighed it down for centuries, without any prospect of relief. How swiftly under those cruel strokes of fortune a people less pliant or less servile would have disappeared from the family of mankind ! There is no chapter in history more pathetic than that which records the rapid extinction of the West Indian aborigines under the harsh and exacting tyranny of their Spanish taskmasters. The negroes, on the contrary, emerged from the darkness of an institution that deprived them of the chief privileges of life, with the original sprightliness and joyousness of their nature undiminished. They are to-day in full possession of all those social qualities that distinguished their remote ancestors, and which have remained unmodified in the race at every subsequent period in spite of the vicissitudes through which it has passed. Among these qualities the most conspicuous still, is a careless and thoughtless good-humor, which, however, can harden into a barbarous cruelty occasionally.

There is another quality which is still more influential in preventing the negro from giving extreme expression to his malicious emotions, namely, his timidity ; as a rule, he is destitute of that manly force of mind which would stimulate him to press forward in a hazardous enterprise without a confusing apprehension of contemporary peril, or that would cause him to meet the shock of that peril, when it comes, with rational firmness. As long as he knows that it is not an immediate accompaniment of an adventure, he is not reluctant to engage in it, for his understanding has little prospective scope. It is a present and not a future risk and jeopardy that he fears. His sensitiveness to danger in one form, as in the commission of a burglary, for example, must, however, be carefully discriminated from his indifference to it in another, as, for instance, in riding an unbroken colt ; his nervous organization seems to be such that all of his sensations of physical pain are dull, and his imagination shows a corresponding heaviness and stolidity, when he is placed in ordinary situations that are likely to result in suffering to himself. It is not the probability of being maimed or killed that disheartens him so much even in a burglarious attempt ; it is rather the uncertainty as to the exact character of the peril which he is confronting, and the moment it may work him harm. Here, too, he has human intelligence and not brute instinct to contend with ; and the darkness surrounding him shakes his resolution by magnifying his terrors.

If the presumption of the negro, when he is disposed to be aggressive in his bearing, is met in a spirit that is prepared, on the instant, to retaliate, he shrinks back with the greatest anxiety for his own safety. And yet the same negro would not hesitate to mount an untamed horse that would dash him to the ground if it could weaken his seat on its back ; and he displays like insensibility when he ascends the scaffold and beholds the awful instruments that are to consummate his impending doom. His eyes are as clear, his hands as steady, and his voice as free from tremor as if he belonged to the mass of disinterested spectators present, instead of being the central figure of the occasion, and, as such, standing upon the edge of the yawning abyss of eternity. There would be an element of sublimity in his patience and serenity here, if these did not have their origin in apathy. He discloses the same obtuseness everywhere else, unless the danger to which he is exposed proceeds directly from the inimical acts of persons. It is largely this fear of a personal conflict that restrains the plantation negro from perpetrating more atrocious crimes than he does, for, amiable as he is, there is a latent ferocity in his nature. That indifference to the suffering of others, which so often causes him, even when unprovoked, to lash his oxen without pity, to kick and maim his faithful dog, and to reprove or strike his children with improper roughness, would be shown still more plainly if he could act under all circumstances with the license of absolute despotism. As he has generally few scruples and little power of self-control, it would be difficult to predict what would be the limit of his excesses when his anger was thoroughly aroused. This is foreshadowed in the character of the requests which he makes of the trick doctors when he seeks the aid of the latter in carrying out his schemes of vengeance ; death is one of the many forms of injury which he desires to inflict through the secret agency of the fatal charms and potions of these trusted and influential impostors.

Entering into a more particularized examination of the criminal record of the blacks, we find that the greater number of the brawls in which individuals of their race are involved among themselves have their incentive in the vehement passions aroused by heated disputes as to proprietorship in women. This is the point of contention which is most frequently raised, and at times it is only settled by a resort to violence as desperate as it is impetuous ; in the struggle no quarter is expected or allowed, and it is only terminated by the hasty retirement or the complete disablement of one of the parties. The final scenes of drunken frolics, too, are often stained with blood, but excepting instances of this kind, in which the negroes are spurred on by their appetites, their quarrels are rarely sanguinary, however licentious the verbal expression given to them. The weapon employed in these frantic assaults is occasionally the razor,[1] which they can wield with a skill and precision as fatal to its victim as it is appalling in the mere physical aspect of the slashing done. They sometimes carry this instrument about their persons unobserved, whipping it out on the most unexpected occasions ; it being an admirable means of attack or defence, because it combines the

---

[1] The razor is used as a weapon by the negroes far oftener in the towns and villages, or along lines of railway, than in the secluded rural districts.

highest effectiveness with the greatest convenience, since it is readily hidden in a small space in the clothing. A sheath-knife is too large to conceal thus, and too awkward to stick in the belt; above all, its appearance is so dangerous that it throws its owner himself into a fright. The aspect of a pistol is still more formidable; it is prudently eschewed for that reason, and properly so, for the negroes, being thoughtless and heedless, are in far more danger of shooting themselves accidentally when they carry such firearms than of implanting a bullet in their adversary. The razor is terrible in execution, but, nevertheless, excites no instinctive apprehension for their lives in the persons handling it.

The negro is not disposed to have affrays with members of the other race, his natural peaceableness being increased in his association with white men by that restraining spirit of subserviency to them which still lingers in his heart. This is disclosed in the fact that it is very rare that he seeks to kill a white man by an open and direct assault. When such a man is murdered, it is, as a rule, the result of a sudden scheme on the part of two or three negroes for the purpose of securing money which they know to be secreted about his person, and the deed is always committed with a degree of atrocity that is unsurpassed in the criminal annals of any country. Even here the negligent character of the race is curiously apparent. The guilty companions do not attempt to remove the various traces of their crime; the act is committed with awkward but relentless coolness and ferocity, the booty is collected, and then the spot is deserted, being left with every evidence of the fatal struggle, including the corpse itself, to bear silent testimony to the awful details of the tragedy of which it has recently been the scene. They do not even endeavor to escape from the neighborhood afterwards, or to take any precaution that will avert suspicion from themselves as the perpetrators of the crime ; on the contrary, they often boldly display articles which they acquired by it, which inevitably implicate them. The final detection of the parties to such crime is always assured, not only because there are so many clues that set the officers upon the proper track, but also because the parties generally confess, in their terror, the moment that they are accused. The total amount of money obtained by most of these murderers for pecuniary gain, is so small a sum that it is surprising that they should run even the risks of ordinary robbery to get possession of it.

Rape is the most frightful crime which the negroes commit against the white people, and their disposition to perpetrate it has increased in spite of the quick and summary punishment that always follows ; and it will be seen that this disposition will grow in proportion as that vague respect which the blacks still entertain for a white skin declines. There is something strangely alluring and seductive to them in the appearance of a white woman ; they are aroused and stimulated by its foreignness to their experience of sexual pleasures, and it moves them to gratify their lust at any cost and in spite of every obstacle. This proneness of the negro is so well understood that the white women of every class, from the highest to the lowest, are afraid to venture to any distance alone, or even to wander unprotected in the immediate vicinity of their homes ; their appreciation of the danger being as keen, and their apprehension of corporal injury as vivid, as if the country were in arms. If it were not for this prudence and .caution on their part, as well as the capital punishment that ensues so swiftly, this crime would be far more frequent than it is. It occurs often enough, however, to inflame the aversion of the white people to the race to a heat that leaves a permanent impression upon their general relations with its members ; and not unnaturally, for rape, indescribably beastly and loathsome always, is marked, in the instance of its perpetration by a negro, by a diabolical persistence and a malignant atrocity of detail that have no reflection in the whole extent of the natural history of the most bestial and ferocious animals. He is not content merely with the consummation of his purpose, but takes that fiendish delight in the degradation of his victim which he always shows when he can reek his vengeance upon one whom he has hitherto been compelled to fear ; and, here, the white woman in his power is, for the time being, the representative of that race which has always overawed him. That this feeling enters largely into the motive of this crime is proven by the fact that he is guilty of it as often against women who are very much advanced in years as against those who have not passed the period of their youth. His invariable impulse after the accomplishment of his purpose is to murder his victim, that being the only means suggested to his mind of escaping the consequence of the act, and this impulse is carried into effect with the utmost barbarity, unless he is accidently interrupted and frightened off.

The average plantation negro does not consider rape to be a very heinous crime. He is so accustomed to the wantonness of the women of his own race that it is not strange that his intellect, having no perception of personal dignity or the pangs of outraged feeling, should be unable to gauge the terrible character of this offense against the integrity of virtuous womanhood, even apart

from the cruel wrong of associating it in such a way
with manhood that is most vile, brutal, and depraved.
The rape of a negress by a male of her own color is almost unheard of, a fact that is a strong proof of the sexual laxness of the plantation women as a class ; for if
they attached any importance to sexual purity, and strenuously resisted all improper encroachment upon it, the
criminal records of the negro men would contain details
of many such assaults.   As it is, their careers are comparatively unblemished in this respect.

The poisoning of persons is not a common crime among
the blacks, perhaps because it is difficult to obtain the
proper substance, there being no noxious herbs in the
local botany from which they can distil what they need,
and at the country stores only the coarsest articles for
the purpose can be purchased.   In the instances of poisoning that occur a female domestic servant is often the
principal party implicated, because she frequently has
access to medicines that are deadly if administered in
large quantities, however harmless when the doses are
small, and she would not hesitate to use these against
master or mistress, or their children, or against individuals of her own race, if she had a fierce impulse of
revenge or resentment to gratify.   The plantation laborers,
on the other hand, generally make use of the torch if
they wish to vent the force of their anger to the detri-
ment of their employer for having offended them.   It is
rare that they go so far as to set fire to the dwelling in
which he lives, but in the privacy of darkness the skulk-
ing incendiaries will enkindle a flame beneath his barns
and cribs, in which the crops of a whole year may be
stowed away, which soon reduces them and their valuable
contents to ashes.   So much fear has the planter of this

laborer : he is not inclined to break into the precincts of his employer's residence, or even into the various divisions of the plantation store, although it contains much that he desires to possess ; it is the watermelon patch, the kitchen-garden, the orchard, the corn pile, the meat house, that are in most danger of his obtrusive fingers. The prospect of these being rifled is constant enough to require a permanent guard for their protection.

So well is this propensity known, that the negroes are not permitted by the planter for whom they may be working to fatten more than two hogs apiece each season. Even two are allowed them with reluctance, because they are provoked to supply these animals with food from the fields of growing corn, the ears being pulled under the cover of darkness, and the deficiency being left to disclose itself in the late autumn when the grain is harvested. As it is, the laborers are tempted, at the proper season for penning pigs, to rob the range of shoats to avoid incurring the expense of purchasing them. When that season arrives, the number of pigs running at large is always very seriously diminished ; and in their capture the rogues must display considerable skill and ingenuity, for they are rarely discovered in the act.

The planters are very much opposed to the owners of the country stores receiving corn in liquidation of debts, as their laborers are stimulated to break into the cribs and barns in order to obtain the grain, with a view to turning it over to the storekeepers, and thus getting a new lease of credit for themselves ; and so strong and emphatic is public sentiment in this respect, that the country merchant who would defy it, would be looked upon as a public enemy, and his custom would fall off in consequence.

The improvidence, as well as the thievishness of the negro is shown in his disposition to steal the rails of the fences that are situated conveniently to his cabin, the seasoned wood, when ignited, affording him that warmth and brilliant light in which he likes to bask. He will not scruple to cut up the most valuable plank for this purpose, or even to tear the dry weather-boarding from his own dwelling, the mere waste which he thus creates being passed over without a thought.

A few of the planters, considering it impossible to restrain the thievishness of their laborers, seek to break its force by entering into a formal agreement with them, that all shall be responsible in pecuniary damages for whatever loss may result from the larcenies of any one ; but the negroes naturally regard this as a harsh and exacting condition, as it involves the innocent with the guilty. Occasionally a planter is found who is stoical and philosophical enough to ignore the thievish acts of his employés, the pecuniary damage entailed being accepted by him as an inevitable part of his debit account, for which he makes the proper pecuniary allowance when he is reckoning his expenses, his irritation venting itself only in a shrug of the shoulder or a muttered imprecation. Many of these petty rogues when discovered slink off the plantation, not because their personal relations with their fellow-laborers become strained and uncomfortable in consequence of the exposure of their guilt, but because they are ashamed to confront their employer, a proof that they are conscious of the impropriety of their behavior. So well aware is that employer and his overseer of this, that they will sometimes pretend to be blind to a theft that is being perpetrated directly under their eyes, if the rogue is a vigorous and industrious hand. To accuse him on the spot is to frighten him into a hasty departure for unknown parts ; to arrest him would occasion a degree of trouble and annoyance that would be out of proportion to the character of the offense ; and to dismiss him would be to create the necessity of hiring another laborer, who would be as easily seduced when tempted to pilfer. Moreover, it would be to expose the inflammable property of the plantation to the torch of a revengeful incendiary.

The public sentiment prevailing among the blacks with respect to the criminal acts of a member of their own race is generally healthy, if the injury inflicted by him falls on one of themselves. Thus they are, as a rule, very much aroused if one negro is slain by another, under aggravated circumstances, and they condemn the murderer with as much severity as the white people ; but as they retain no mental impressions for any length of time, their anger and hostility soon subside into comparative obliviousness of the deed. This is also true of their feeling with respect to crimes that are much less heinous and atrocious. There is no public opinion among them, however, that uncompromisingly reprobates an individual of their own color who is guilty of a violation of the law, however gross, from which white people alone suffer. Even a capital offense like murder or rape, of which a white man or woman has been the victim, awakens no overwhelming horror in their breasts, by the mere force of a common humanity. The shock which information of such a crime produces is not one of spontaneous indignation ; and if such a shock is experienced at all, it soon declines into a disinterested curiosity. So far from always wishing to assist in the arrest of any one of their fellows, who has made himself liable to punishment by an act of incendiarism or burglary, which has resulted in a very serious pecuniary damage to a white proprietor, they often seek by every secret means to aid him to escape. Instead of showing disapproval of his crime, by an attitude of eagerness to prevent him from getting away, they frequently become active accessories to it, after the fact, by their anxiety to forward his deliverance from danger. A curious freemasonry obtains among them, under these circumstances, which is voluntarily and passionately sustained by a whole community of plantation negroes, uniting them, old and young alike, in a conspiracy to protect the criminal, by throwing his pursuers off the scent. The great mass is never so plainly observed to be influenced by a common impulse as in such a juncture as this. No political felon in a conquered country, whose boldness has endeared him to the hearts of his people, but exposed him to imprisonment at the hands of the alien authorities, was ever silently and surreptitiously befriended with more ardor than such a burglar or incendiary thus out of the pale of the law; who throws himself upon the good offices of his race. In the instance of an offense like petit larceny, the negroes occasionally show openly the sympathy that they feel for any one of their companions whose guilty part in it has been proven. They certainly do not always avoid him as a man who has sunk to a low point of shame and degradation ; on the contrary, they sometimes conduct themselves towards him as if they thought that he had been dealt with harshly, and was therefore entitled to their pity, his only fault, apparently, being that he was so unfortunate or so awkward as to be discovered. There can

be no hope of any improvement in their public sentiment with respect to this, their most common violation of
the law, until there has been an accumulation of property
among them.   As they acquire valuable articles of various
kinds, they will be more solicitous that the rights of ownership shall be strictly respected, and such a wholesome
opinion as this, brought into play among the members of
the best class by the mere force of utility and selfishness,
may permeate in time to those of the worst, and thus influence the general body to look upon larceny as inex-
cusable.   As to the sentiment relative to such crimes as
murder, rape, and arson, there can be no prospect of an
advance until the moral tone of the whole race has been
elevated, if time shall show that it is capable of being
elevated.

VII.

RELIGION.

THE negro is remarkable for a very devout spirit, so far as this signifies a passionate religious feeling in contradistinction to sober and godly conduct ; as an abstract hope and a naked aspiration, it colors his whole nature as much as his most impetuous appetites do. There is a touch of pathos even in its most ordinary disclosure, however inconsistent with the practice of his life, because it has all the simplicity and directness of sincerity. It seems to be common to individuals of his race belonging to every period of life. The child left alone in the cabin, or sent off to a distance on an errand, is heard singing hymns with almost as much fervor and devotion as a recent convert at a revival ; and a girl who has not reached the marriageable age will fall into as much extravagance during the progress of the services at church as the most vigorous and susceptible of the elderly women. In the hearts of the young and old alike, religion strikes a chord that responds with equal promptness and fulness in all.

It is not confined to sex ; the man is as devout as the woman, being as much open to religious impressions and as much dominated by his religious emotions, although their influence does not cause him to act as wildly and hysterically as she does, for, on the whole, he is more able to control himself, and yet his deportment, when he is full of the transport and ecstasy of religious happiness, is much more apt to transfix the attention of the observer, because his frame is larger and more robust. To see it shaking with childish agitation seems to be so strangely out of keeping with its maturity and strength as to amount almost to a phenomenon.

This religious feeling of the negroes is not restricted to any particular time or special locality. They carry it into every situation and every employment. The greater number of their songs, and these run over the whole gamut of their aspirations and emotions, are hymns that embody their spiritual hopes in monotonous rhythm, rude language, and disconnected sentences. The liveliest of the plantation ditties, even, have a religious echo. Those melodies that roll over the harvest fields as the long line of gleaners gather the severed wheat into shocks, or that are borne far and wide on the frosty air when the corn is being shucked by the light of the November moon, have a subtle tone, even when the words are lewd or jovial, that is expressive of that profound sadness that trembles in the refrains of the hymns. The plowman as he urges on his team in the act of breaking up the sod, the carter perched upon the top of his loaded wagon on the way to the granary, the hand at work among the plants in the tobacco lot, the scytheman in the clover, the herdsman in the pasture, the woodman in the forest, the boatman standing at the helm as his craft drops down the stream,—wherever and whenever, in short, the occupation of the negro secludes him either for a short or a long time, from the companionship of his race, he will often relieve his loneliness by singing with a devout and melancholy intonation. And this is peculiar to no hour and to no season. As he goes forth in all the beauty, freshness, and joy of a vernal morning, the same long-drawn but mournful sounds will frequently issue from his lips that are heard from them as he plods towards his cabin through the chill and dreary December dusk ; he will sing the same sorrowful notes at midday when the world is flooded with cheerful light, that he pours forth upon the bosom of the darkness as he passes through the fields and woods on his way from one settlement of his people to another. Whether, indeed, he is returning from a wedding or a funeral, a political mass-meeting or a revival, his voice is apt to break out in that dismal chant, to which the hymns of the race have been sung immemorially, and which is not without a touch of grandeur in its solemnity.

It is one of the most marked peculiarities of the negro that although he is very cheerful in his social instincts and bright in his temper, his religious spirit, nevertheless, is more lugubrious than that of the most austere and embittered Puritanism. The sunniness of his general disposition is reflected in his view of every thing that interests him, and in the whole tenor of his conduct, except in his system of belief (whether religious or superstitious) and manner of worship. As soon as his thoughts revert to religion, an ominous cloud seems to rise and darken his mind ; he gropes in shadows that are constantly assuming different shapes to increase his disturbance. A heavy burden now rests upon his heart, under all other circumstances so animated and so blithe, which he cannot ease or remove ; his soul is penetrated with sadness ; his whole being seems to be transfused into one overwhelming emotion of sorrow. Few rays of brightness, indeed, reach him from that heaven which is pictured upon his imagination with such minute and

vivid perfection of detail. For although his religion is a
hope, it has little of the joy of hope except at the height
of a spiritual paroxysm ; in his ordinary life it is full of
an agitating fear, but this fear is not based on any consciousness of depravity that forces upon his mind a
doubt as to the certainty of election. " I am going to
heaven when I die," is a song of confidence and triumph
which has its echo in the breasts of every negro upon
whose ears its familiar words of happiness fall. No individual is apprehensive of the contrary in his own instance. His gaze does not waver in the clearness of its
perception of the material aspects of the hereafter, and
no cloud of skepticism ever rises in his soul, and wholly
shuts that fair vision of the city of eternal life from
sight. It is merely the mystery of physical death, to
him the most interesting and fascinating of all natural
phenomena, that causes him to pause, and from that he
shrinks not so much with cowardice as with morbid awe.
It repels him, and yet it attracts him. Strongly inclined
as the members of his race are to confine their attention
to the present, and especially indisposed as they are to
look forward to the future, the thought of death is not
absent for a great length of time from their minds. They
linger around a dying companion far more curious in
their observation of the stages of dissolution than keenly
aware of the great loss that is so soon to fall on them in
the passing away of a friend ; they fix their eyes upon
his countenance with breathless emotion, and sway from
side to side, and moan as he passes into the last article.
Of all the various individuals in the precincts of the
cabin, the dying person is perhaps the only one unmoved ;
now that the end of his life is close upon him, the fear
that he had felt is probably dispelled, and he sinks

into unconsciousness with pious ejaculations or with profound indifference and stolidity.

There is rarely an element of sublimity, however, in the deportment of the negro under these solemn circumstances ; he does not often exhibit here a clear understanding and a firm spirit that, recognizing the whole character of the situation, with all in it that tends to excite the greatest alarm, yet rises superior to it by the force of an intrepidity that cannot be made to tremble or to falter. The negro yields to the inevitable, not with a philosophy that leans upon its own strength alone for support, nor with that spirit which discovers in every juncture the aptness and justness of the theory that "whatever is, is right," or the revelation that "all things work for good," but rather with a resignation that banishes intelligence, and an apathy that does not allow one ray of light to enter the soul. It is in this mood that he generally submits himself to the certain issue of the last contest with death ; and he shows the same state of mind whether he is struck down by a sudden accident when in full health, or is to gradually decline to his last sigh, under the insidious attacks of old age or disease. Religion may smooth the gradations of that decline, but only occasionally illuminates the last scene with the serene glow of a steady and discriminating faith.

The religious emotions that sway the blacks at their funerals and revivals and in their churches, are merely a physical drunkenness ; a species of excitement, indeed, that resembles the effect of over-indulgence in liquor, the fumes of which, rising to the brain, produce an exaltation of feeling that is expressed in vehement movements of the body, ecstatic laughter, and boisterous singing. It is long, however, before this agitation exhausts the physical powers. At its height, it seems to increase the bodily vigor tenfold, inflaming it with the passionate energy of madness. A negress in a religious paroxysm acts as though she were endowed with superhuman strength, however frail or emaciated she may be. Several men are required to prevent her from laying violent hands on herself, and in the struggle that ensues, she will toss them about very roughly.

When we seek the cause of this transport, which is exhibited in different degrees by all, we find it to be most elusive. It is not grief, since those who create the greatest disturbance at the open grave are rarely the nearest relatives or the closest friends of the deceased ; it is not consciousness of depravity, for this transport is not always attended by a confession of personal wickedness, even at a revival. It does not spring from an acknowledgment of the omnipotence of God, nor from a recognition of the uncertainty of life, nor even from a vivid apprehension of death. It originates in none of these things wholly, and yet all, perhaps, enter into their state of mind in the beginning, whether they are aware of it or not ; after the emotion has once gained possession, it carries them to such an extreme that they lose all definite idea of the character of their own feelings. Their excitement when it reaches this point has sunk into an ordinary fit of mania. Whatever its origin, it is obvious that the excitement itself is opposed to true religious feeling, being, in some measure, only sensual gratification. Their eager and susceptible natures, overcome by a desire for change and amusement, have recourse to this morbid and unwholesome means of arousing the emotions, which, however sombre, titillate their unrefined sensibilities agreeably. The negro has an incorrect idea of religion, not because he has been instructed wrongly, when he has been instructed at all, but because no kind of information that relates to his conduct makes a permanent impression on his mind in opposition to his passions and appetites. He undoubtedly grasps what may be termed the picturesque parts of religion, such, for instance, as the existence, beyond the grave, of a material abode for those who shall be saved, as well as for those who shall be damned. In other words, he comprehends clearly the hereafter as a mere prolongation of this life. Few races, indeed, even if we include those as ignorant and uncivilized, have such an abiding conception of a spiritual future as the African, wherever found ; but, on the other hand, none disconnect that future so distinctly and so absolutely from all that is done on earth as its members do, even when they have been educated under influences more or less refining. The religion of the plantation negro is a code of belief, and not a code of morals, having no real connection with the practical side of his existence, and slight bearing on the common motives of his conduct. The sermons delivered in the churches of his race have little reference to self-government in fundamental moral details, both because the congregations would resent any pointed reflection upon their special failings, and because the average preacher himself does not comprehend that there is any close relation between religion and practical morality. Breathe a practical spirit into the services, and these become dull and prosaic to their minds at once. Within the precincts of their sacred edifices they wish to hear of heaven ; they are impatient of homilies which, if obeyed, would cut them off from the enjoyment of all the loose pleasures that vary their daily existence. As they gather under the humble roofs of their churches, they are like men and women who, aware that it will not be long before they will have to set out on a journey to a distant country which they have never visited, but from which they will never return, are anxious to be informed of its character, but without clearly recognizing that there are any ties between that country and their own, or that any thing that they now do can prevent them from arriving in it at last.   So little stress, on the whole, do they lay upon practical morality, that they are generally indifferent as to whether the preachers, elders, and deacons of the various congregations to which they belong are circumspect in their lives or not.   Of all the representative men to be found among the negroes, the least estimable, in some respects, are those who fill these clerical and official positions ; the explanation of this being that the occupants of such positions are selected not because justness of temper, purity of spirit, and propriety of conduct point them out as fitted to be the best exemplars of their people, but because they are men of more firmness and decision of character.   The fact that they have these traits, instead of always signifying that they are more upright and honorable, frequently means that they are more unscrupulous, because less under the domination of fear, and more dangerous, because more resolute in enforcing their will.   Unfortunately, too many are inclined to use their influence and power simply to carry out their selfish purposes, or to administer to their physical appetites. However far or openly these may transgress every law of pure conduct, it does not invariably follow that a protest is raised by the members of their congregations ; no act on their part, however open to condemnation, leading inevitably to their deposition amid a storm of contempt, disgust, or indignation. Even detection in a theft, a partnership in a felony, exposure in a lewd escapade, public drunkenness, are unhappily too frequently passed over as leaving no ineffaceable stain upon their official and personal reputations.

Entertaining an opinion as lenient as this of the bad conduct of their highest spiritual officers, it may well be supposed that the members of the church are not as strict as they should be in judging themselves, when they too fall into gross irregularities of behavior. The most pious among them are too often those who are the laxest in their daily lives, and the most unrestrained in their ordinary deportment ; a strong religious feeling being apparently consistent with the lowest instincts and the most unbridled passions. The sublimest faith, because simple and unquestioning, like the faith of a little child, is found in them, associated with a profound insensibility to every principle upon which religion rests, and without the observance of which it is the hollowest of mockeries ; indeed the religious, as distinguished from the moral, sense is frequently seen to be as fully developed in a negro imprisoned for murder, or arson, or burglary, or even rape, as in those who are comparatively blameless. A colored felon is very apt when standing on the scaffold to display the intensity and vividness of the religious sentiment in his heart, although the dark stains of a demoniacal crime may yet linger upon his hands. Not a doubt crosses his mind as to his spiritual destination. Heaven, with all its transcendent pleasures and glories, opens on his sight even before he closes his eyes to the spectacle of that earth which would be but a scene of godless anarchy if abandoned to men as unrestrained and wicked as himself. And this spirit is not begotten by the enthusiasm of a sudden repentance as vehement as his position is fatal ; it has always lurked in the central recesses of his being, and has, no doubt, been exhibited with equal violence at many previous times, when his sensibilities were deeply touched by wild appeals to his religious nature.

We find the same inconsistent spirit running through the whole mass of the race ; a skeptic or scoffer among its members would be branded as an outlaw, who would be summarily dealt with if he ventured to obtrude his opinions on a prominent occasion. Not even a difference of political sentiment would separate a negro so quickly and so far from his friends and companions as infidelity. Such a state of mind, however, is wholly foreign to the intellectual leaning of his people, for their turn of thought is never speculative.

That the negro can be so full of religious faith at the very time that his conduct is so palpably opposed to true piety, is largely due to the fact that he has that extreme inability to appreciate and measure the practical relations of things that we observe in children, as well as their lack of logical power. And then, too, he acts precisely as his religion impels him, without stopping a moment to inquire why he does so. It has all the force of an appetite which he cannot control whether he desires to do so or not. He follows unquestionably wherever it leads, and it never relaxes its hold upon him, being associated with a free indulgence of instincts that are apparently in conflict with it, because it is as much an instinct as these are. He does not recognize that there is any relation between his various physical appetites ; and his religious instinct is as disconnected from his physical appetites as one of the latter is from the rest. It goes hand in hand with them, but rarely runs counter to them ; there being no more incongruity to his mind between his religious impulse and his lewdness, for instance, than between his lewdness and his hunger and thirst. Each one colors and shapes his conduct according to circumstances. The result is, that his conversion, as a rule, does not mean regeneration in the Christian sense—that is, such an alteration of character as will lead him at least to try to repress his bad inclinations and passions. That is not the condition usually superinduced in him ; it is only a burst of enthusiasm, a temporary state of intellectual drunkenness that has no practical bearing on the general spirit of his life. This fact in the history of one person is illustrated on a still greater scale in the history of a community, which is a mere aggregation of similar individuals. A wave of emotional excitement sweeps over a whole neighborhood, arousing the negroes to frenzy ; there is a universal wail of unhappiness, followed by a shout, as a triumphant expression of eternal security through faith, and yet no special change is observed in the course of the community afterwards, not even in a short period immediately succeeding these revivals.

The divorce between religion and morality in the life of the negro fills the observer at first with astonishment, for it seems impossible that he can be both devout and depraved at the same moment, but if he is suspected in the beginning, of hypocrisy, that suspicion is dispelled after a brief association with him. It is true that he is not lacking in capacity for dissimulation, as is frequently disclosed in his personal relations with the whites ; nevertheless, it is doubtful whether he could play a hypocritical part for any length of time, for the reason that it is not practicable for him to carry out, with unswerving steadiness of will, any purpose that requires an unremitting watch over his natural impulses and a resolute repression of them when they rise. He finds it hard, too, to remain long enough in one state of mind to continue to desire to realize even the wishes that can be accomplished at one stroke, much less those that are dependent for success upon an extended and intricate course of action. For these reasons, as well as because his temperament is innately devotional, he cannot be charged with religious cant and pretense, however immoral or criminal he may be.

At the very time that he overlooks the union of immorality of conduct with holiness of thought in himself, it is probable that his conscience would condemn him severely, if he were to take part in any kind of amusement. Some devout individuals of his race, for instance, regard mere secular pleasures, such as singing and dancing, as far more serious offenses against the Christian spirit than larceny or unchastity. They would prefer, as members of the Church, to be caught in the act of pilfering rather than in a performance on the fiddle or in a breakdown ; and would rather be exposed as guilty of adultery, than to have their allegiance to mere religious canons questioned. This is simply the outgrowth of the fact, to which allusion has already been made, that the essential and fundamental principles of religion amount only, with the plantation negroes, to a system of belief. As long as they shall adhere to that system as firmly and honestly as they now do, it will be impossible to charge them with hypocrisy. This stickling for the hollow rules of religion seems strange, when all its practical lessons are ignored ; but the mere anxiety which they display, in sustaining these rules, is a proof at once of their sincerity and their obtuseness.

Owing to the passionate and emotional bent of their natures, the negroes have never been in sympathy with the Episcopal church, even when their moral and mental characters have been more or less refined. The restriction of its services to a certain set form, and its steady discouragement of all vehement expression of the feelings, strip religion, according to their view, of every thing that makes it vital and realistic ; its essence evaporating because that spirit which exalts the worshippers with ecstasy, and fills them with uncontrollable enthusiasm, has no room for display. It is this desire to give full rein to all the promptings of their religious fervor that causes the system of government that distinguishes the Baptist denomination to be considered with so much favor by the individuals of the race ; and with this church, in consequence, the great majority are connected. Its ceremony of immersion particularly is full of meaning to their minds ; the vast crowd, swaying, shouting, and gesticulating, the strange and picturesque local details of the vicinity, the canopy of sky and cloud overhead, the late hour, the emotional rites, all tending to impress the occasion upon which they are received into the bosom of that church most deeply on their minds. The moment from which their souls are made safe from damnation is thus distinctly marked in time, their admission to the fold being celebrated with a tumultuous display, worthy of such a supreme event in their lives. To whatever religious denomination the blacks may claim to belong, however, they always breathe their peculiar emotional temper into its sacred observances. Most frequently they are only nominally mem-

bers of a church organization, so inclined are they to act
upon their own devotional impulses in defiance of definite
customs and conventionalities of every kind. It is largely
owing to this dislike of restraint that they show such an
unmistakable desire and determination to worship alone
to themselves. In all of the churches of the white people before the late war there were galleries set apart
exclusively for such of the slaves as wished to attend the
services, and these galleries used to be well filled every
Sunday, but that is not the case now. A stranger entering one of these churches as they are to-day perceives at
once that the room allowed for the accommodation of
the worshippers is too great for the number of people
present. The explanation of this is that the section of
the floor which is reserved for the negroes is always
vacant. Why do they stay away? It is not on account
of the attitude of the white people toward them, for both
clergymen and congregations would be pleased for them
to come, and would put themselves to much trouble to
induce them to do so, if any step that could be taken
with that view would avail. The reason is to be found
elsewhere. In the first place, the blacks absent themselves because their confinement to special benches re-
minds them of their social inferiority and subordination.
It recalls too the days of slavery, and they are impatient
of every thing that does so. In addition to this, the
average white clergyman speaks above the level of their
intelligence, or deals with the sacred themes in a way
not congenial to their temperaments. Above all, and
this is explanation enough in itself, they do not feel
at ease there, and cannot conduct themselves as their
emotions impel them. These churches are a part of the
social organization of the whites, and are almost as

closely associated with their lives as their nurseries, chambers, and drawing-rooms. The negroes know that they are as much shut out of this social circle as if they were still slaves, and they shrink away from it instinctively in consequence. In their own churches they can act as their feelings prompt them to act, conscious all the while that they are not scrutinized by critical or laughing eyes. There they can allow both bodies and souls to run riot. Does the power of the religious spirit cause them to spring involuntarily to their feet and shout in an ecstasy? Then, they are sure of the pity, sympathy, and admiration of all in earshot. The old hymns that console or elate them so much are sung by the white people to various and difficult tunes. The negroes, on the other hand, roll these hymns from their breasts to one simple metre which is full of the emphatic fervor of their ardent emotions. It is this portion of the services that touches their sensibilities most keenly. They look upon themselves as having so little part in the churches of their employers, and they feel so little interest in the services there, that even when it is their duty to drive the families of the planters thither on Sunday, they rarely enter, preferring to remain outside instead, and gossip until the congregations reappear. The overtures which the white clergymen make to the blacks are met coldly and reluctantly, if these overtures are with the view to the formation of any continuous and permanent religious association with them.[1] They are not unwilling, however, to hear sermons from such clergymen occasionally, if the latter are careful to preach at an hour when they will not interfere with the services of the colored pastors, who are very jealous of their prerogative. Perfect de-

[1] That is, as their pastors.

corum distinguishes an audience gathered together under these circumstances. Only a few hours before, it is probable that its members had been in a state of tumultuous religious excitement, but now they listen quietly and attentively. Each man and woman feel that they must bear themselves in the presence of a white person of consideration with proper reserve, if they wish to retain his respect, and they are as anxious to do so as so many children put upon their good behavior by the promise of a reward. The clergyman, however, avoids playing too long upon their emotions, and he knows at once that he is doing so if the old men in the congregation begin faintly to groan and the women to sway from side to side on the benches.

In consequence of the disposition of the negroes to withdraw to themselves in their religious worship, we find that their church organizations reflect their social as well as their religious spirit. With them, indeed, the church is as much a social as a religious institution. It is especially remarkable as being the only form of organization that the blacks have been able to sustain with a steady and unchanging concurrence of mind, for it is in the one matter of co-operation that they have always shown in their general affairs the greatest element of weakness, being unable, usually, to work soberly and persistently together for a common object. This same weakness would, no doubt, be displayed in the church organization if its purposes were wholly practical but these purposes are mixed, such as are practical being subordinate to pleasure and religion. As a mere institution, however, it undoubtedly gives head to the various inclinations of the negroes, infusing all the vigor of a co-operative body, large in numbers and united by the closest sympathies, into their ordinary social and political tendencies.

The church, as an organization, is growing in strength and popularity with the members of the race. One evidence of this is the fact that even the congregations in the most remote and barren regions are being more and more supplied with preachers who are supported wholly by the contributions of their charges, thus relieving them of the necessity of manual labor. The educated minister is thrusting the uneducated from his pulpit, but his influence, on the whole, has not been more beneficial than that of the old-fashioned plantation preacher, who, however far he may depart from the path of a pure and upright life, is, at least, a firm and fervent believer in the truth of religion. Nor is he contemptible as a mere orator. Gifted with remarkable fluency, he can often run with true oratorical skill over the whole gamut of emotions. He speaks very frequently with such genuine power that the ungrammatical language in which his sermons are couched is forgotten. There is at times, too, a striking aptness and picturesqueness of illustration in his speech, a use of racy similes and metaphors drawn from his observation of the fields and forests, and its manifold and ever changing forms of life, or from his personal experience in those lowly walks of existence in which all of his days have run.

The educated preacher, on the other hand, is frequently so ambitious and artificial in his style that he is unintelligible both to himself and his audience. Having a smattering of theology, he is disposed to be learned, dogmatic, and pompous in his discourse, confining himself to knotty and abstruse doctrines that do not relate to practical life ; and in consequence he communicates to the members of his congregation little of that enthusiasm which, under the old ministrations, would spread like a rapid contagion among them, throwing them into a state of uncontrollable excitement on the smallest provocation. The influence of the average preacher of the new school is not as useful in personal intercourse as it might be. The little knowledge that he has acquired has probably puffed him up very much in his bearing without strengthening his principles, and the inflation of his egotism has perhaps only deepened his selfishness. The cultivation of his mind, in making him more keen-witted, has not necessarily made him more scrupulous and con-scientious. His power over the individuals of his race is supreme, and it is too often exercised to his own per-sonal advantage, both in a social and political way. In him, too, we discover the first trace of religious hypocrisy in the negro.

With such men as these at the head of their churches, men remarkable, at the best, for comparative ignorance and, at the worst, for the grossest corruption of spirit, it is impossible for the religious associations of the blacks, as constituted at present, to subserve with much success the purpose of improving their moral tendencies. The character of such men is just now but a reflection of the character of the associations themselves. Even the good that the latter accomplish is so largely mixed with evil that there can be little doubt that the negroes of most communities would be in a better condition if they had no separate churches of their own at all.

VIII.

SUPERSTITION.

THERE is no peculiarity of the negro that is more marked in its influence on his conduct than his superstitiousness, and in the individual of no other race is the same trait more fully developed. It has its origin in the obtuseness and narrowness of his intellect and the alertness and gloominess of his imagination. Like a child, he dwells as much in a visionary world as in the material world ; he is constantly passing in thought the debatable ground that divides the natural from the supernatural, and he is unconscious of the stage of transition, for his spirit moves with as much freedom in the domain of the one as in that of the other. His perceptions seem to be as much unobstructed there as here, and his foothold as sure and unhesitating. There is, however, no touch of poetry, or element of tenderness or benignity in the general character of this superstitiousness ; the forces which it calls into play are callous and sinister ; all cheerfulness is banished from the atmosphere in which it flourishes, and only malice, hatred, mischief, and calamity remain. As in the instance of his religion, the native sunniness of his disposition does not irradiate this atmosphere with its own light ; his mind, as soon as it enters it, becomes at once dejected, or is darkened by the gravest apprehensions. The vivid gayety of his ordinary temper causes the reaction from joy to terror to be the more extreme, his susceptibility to the one emotion being attended by an equal susceptibility to the other, although at the opposite pole.   Every aspect of that world, which is material only in his morbid fancy, is calculated to awe, frighten, and repel him ; and, in consequence, he lives at a greater tension in this insubstantial sphere of existence than he does in the substantial even ; indeed, the conception which he has of this unreal world is much more distinct than that which he has of the real, because it only appeals to him through emotions which make the deepest impression on his mind.   His superstition, in fact, is so dense that it would be more correct to say that he does not distinguish this incorporeal sphere at all from that in which he breathes and moves.   His thoughts revert to it so frequently that it is surprising that it does not destroy his happiness completely ; and it would certainly do so but for the characteristic inability of the negro to retain any one notion or feeling continuously enough to influence his conduct permanently.

Spirits enter more largely into the superstition of the negro than any other figment of the imagination ; he has comparatively few of those isolated fancies that constitute a disconnected system of belief with many less credulous peoples.   His superstition, on the contrary, has an overshadowing personal element in it, and of an evil bent ; perhaps because on his native continent it was man whom he had most reason to fear, and therefore it was man of whom he stood in most dread.   He came finally to regard the spirit dislodged from the body with the same emotions.   His conviction as to the existence of this spirit after death cannot be shaken, and to his disordered view it is constantly assuming a visible shape, but rarely, if ever, that form of flesh and blood which it once inhabited. This shape is shadowy and grisly, and always aggressive. The ghosts of his nearest and most amiable friends seem to raise as much alarm in his breast as the spectres of his most violent and resolute enemies. When animals reappear in these visions, they are presented, as a rule, as they were in life, for he has not the same vivid conception of the spirit of a horse, dog, or ox that he has of the spirit of one of his own species. It is remarkable that, although he believes so firmly in ghosts, and associates them with the most prominent spots in his vicinity, yet this does not always prevent him from wandering even at the darkest hour, amid scenes that he has often asserted to be haunted. It is probable that he will avoid a graveyard after sunset, but he will, perhaps, do so for the reason that might influence a white man, namely, the thoughts which it suggests are dismal or uncanny ; and yet he will often enter a deep wood or cross a lonely field in the midst of the forest, while hardly a ray from the dim stars in a moonless sky penetrates an occasional opening in the black clouds overhead. He will frequently walk many miles after nightfall to idle away a few hours at the plantation store ; and after relating many tales of his own encounters with spectres at various periods in his life, will return to his distant cabin along a path that runs over hill and down valley, with a dense growth of trees and shrubs on either side, in apparent indifference to the dangers that are supposed to beset his way. And if he has an amorous tryst to keep with some local Venus, he will defy a legion of the ghosts of his deceased acquaintances in order to be punctual to the hour appointed.

It is the spirit that he cannot see rather than the one that he can see that impresses itself most deeply on his imagination. He can roughly measure the ability of ghost to harm him, as well as anticipate with more or less exactness the manner in which it will strike, and the moment at which it will, but both the presence and the intentions of a spirit that never makes itself visible are all the more terrible because not precisely known or knowable. As a modification of this, the negro dreads the malevolence of persons whom he believes to be endowed with supernatural power, and who, therefore, stand upon the footing of a spirit, whether visible or invisible. Here, again, the personal element in his superstition is apparent. That original fear which he had of man, as having the physical strength as well as the desire to inflict injury, which also entered into his view of the spirit after death, he still entertains of certain men as gifted not with physical vigor, for that is now unimportant, but with a subtle and occult skill that has no reflection in nature. In other words, he is convinced that there are individuals who can carry out by supernatural means various schemes of mischief or ruin without the possibility of being thwarted. He has an unquestioning faith in the art of witchcraft, a form of superstition that prevails universally among his fellows, overshadowing every other, and differing very little in character and exhibition from the variety of superstition that flourishes on the west coast of Africa to-day among the descendants of ancestors who are common to the American negro also. His retention of this superstition after the lapse of such a great length of time, passed in the midst of different local surroundings and amid the most modifying influences, is one of the strongest proofs of the inherent tenacity of the fundamental qualities of his race. Plantation negroes, in a convenient distance of churches, schools, and railroads, are found to have as firm a belief in witchcraft as those savages of the African bush who file their teeth, perforate the cartilage of their noses, and expose their bodies without a strip of clothing. They do not offer up bloody sacrifices as they do in Hayti ; they have not adopted any ceremonial like that of the Voodoo, but the spirit of their superstition is nevertheless the same as that of the West Indian and Congo blacks, and from its vigor and intensity it is not improbable that if they were abandoned to themselves it would in time be displayed in rites similar to those observed in Guinea and the Haytian Republic.   There are communities of negroes in the tobacco belt of Virginia to-day that so far resemble an African tribe as to have a professional trick doctor, a man whose only employment, and therefore whose only means of earning his living, lies in the practice of the art of witchcraft, but it is probable that he is an unconscious empiric as a rule.[1]   Like all the influential men of his race, he is apt to be an individual of unusual force of will and decision of purpose, and enjoying as such a certain power irrespective of his representative character ; clothed with the additional dignity of such a character, his authority meets with no opposition except from those who are playing the same part.

A trick doctor is invested with even more importance than a preacher, since he is regarded with the respect that fear excites, and not unnaturally, for while he is as impartial as an ordinary physician, his art is often employed to inflict injury.   This imparts a terrific aspect

[1] The trick doctor does not generally remain long in any one community, but passes from neighborhood to neighborhood in the pursuit of his profession.

to his character, a fact of which he is keenly aware, for he is observed to be eager to turn the position which he occupies to his own advantage and profit. It is doubtful, indeed, whether a negro could follow a more lucrative pursuit. The members of his race, being very extravagant, are ready to lavish all that they have to attain an end, especially if it relates to the gratification of their evil passions. It is frequently in connection with these that they seek the aid of such a pretender ; and he does not respond to their requests unless he is remunerated for his services. The profession is not broken down by competition, because it is rare that a negro has the boldness to adopt it, so much in awe of witchcraft do the blacks stand, and so anxiously do they shrink from meddling with what is so occult and dangerous. The daily conduct of a trick doctor, even when not engaged in the work of his profession, is more or less secretive and retiring ; he does not associate as unreservedly with his fellows as he would do if he made no claim to such mysterious skill ; on the contrary, he is inclined to withdraw from the crowd, and in doing so, to surround himself with every thing that is likely to impress the imagination of his dupes. His intercourse with mere individuals is constant, but it is almost wholly in a professional way. The fact that he is indisposed to enter into that free intercourse which prevails among the individuals of his race is due not only to his wish to sustain his prestige, but very probably also to his consciousness that the part he is playing is one of such dignity that he should be careful not to lower it by too much familiarity.

The trick doctor is simply a man who employs the arts of the Obeah practitioners together with the arts of the Myal. In the West Indies, as well as in Africa, these two sects are broadly distinguished from each other, one aim of the Myal being to combat the designs of the followers of Obeah, whose usual purpose is to inflict and revenge injuries. The priests of Myalism also hold themselves out as medicine men. A plantation trick doctor pretends to these various powers, and in his ordinary practice, acts as if he possessed them all. Thus, for instance, he is sought by negroes who wish a spell to be cast upon those who have aroused their vindictive feelings ; and he complies with the request by transferring an article of a trivial nature either inside or to the immediate vicinity of the cabins of the victims, who recognize the medium of the art at once, from their intimate knowledge of the sort of material that is always used.

Again, when a negro is convinced that he has been tricked, but not by a plantation doctor, his impulse is to obtain the assistance of the latter if at hand, and his fear is only removed when a counteracting influence has been brought to bear. And still more often too, when individuals of his race are sick, believing that their illness is due to a similar cause, although that illness is exhibited in a perfectly natural way, and its origin is obvious and palpable, they will call in a trick doctor, in preference to the regular practitioner of the neighborhood, and in consequence, they often die under his care, as no proper means are adopted to arrest the progress of the disease. On the other hand, there are cases of sickness among them, that are more readily treated by a trick doctor than by a licensed physician, for what is needed is a soothing stimulant for the mind and not the administration of a dose to the body. The cures that he will effect in instances of this kind seem almost miraculous, the process of recuperation being so rapid as to be inexplicable but for the fact that the disease is not physical but mental. The influence of the trick doctor is sustained without any loss of prestige, owing to the susceptibility of the mind of the individual negro to these strange impressions as well as its responsiveness to the remedy. Let the latter be convinced that he is bewitched, and he will sink at once into despondency; his figure droops, his face becomes clouded and sad, while his general health declines; from the condition of a vigorous man, animated by the liveliest and most buoyant spirits, he passes into an unwholesome melancholy, which, preying upon his vitality soon reduces him to a state of prostration. Occasionally, however, this despair inflames rather than saps his physical energies; he is like one attacked by madness, acting as wildly as if he had not only been deprived of his wits but was possessed of a devil. He falls into paroxysms of anger alternating with fits of fear; even in intervals of comparative peace of mind, he cannot remain quiet owing to the disturbing character of his thoughts.

The phenomenon of his restoration to health is almost as remarkable. His first anticipation that he can be cured, causes a sudden revulsion of joy as soon as it is realized, and as the stages of recuperation advance towards a complete recovery, confidence takes the place of doubt and anxiety; the expression of his countenance changes from sorrow to happiness; his form becomes erect once more; his old manner is resumed; he mingles freely and cordially with his friends and acquaintances; and the whole of the severe episode through which he has recently passed, is apparently forgotten.

A neighborhood in which a trick doctor may happen to be, is sometimes thrown into a state of general turmoil

by his presence ; it then resembles a community of personal enemies whose hands strike at each other either
directly, or through the medium of his supposed power.
He acts as a secret agent for gratifying all the animosi-
ties that find lodgment in their breasts, thus allowing
them to reek their ill-feelings with absolute immunity.
It is one of the most remarkable traits of the negroes
that they have no compunction about inflicting injury
when they can do so slyly, and safely ; the presence of a
trick doctor affords them an ample opportunity for the
display of this characteristic, for witchcraft is as furtive
a means of doing harm as poison or the torch. All their
evil passions seem to be aroused in these periods of
occasional excitement. There is a notable increase of
quarrelling and wrangling among them ; emotions of
hatred and revenge are stimulated ; ominous threats and
deep imprecations fill the air ; the whole atmosphere is
alive with anger and terror. Many individuals of both
sexes are either bent upon damaging or destroying, or
they are on the alert to detect evidences that they
themselves are falling victims to those sinister influences
that they are ready to employ against others without
hesitation, but which they dread so much when directed
against themselves. They discover signs on every side
that portend extreme calamity to them ; the smallest
and most insignificant objects are invested with a profound meaning ; things weak and trivial in themselves
are symbols of a power as diffusive as the universe and
as unscrupulous as hell ; the world that moves so orderly
in its grooves has apparently fallen into the hands of
malignant forces ; the very sky itself is darkened with
a cloud of evil ; all nature has succumbed to malicious
spirits.

There have been occasions when so much agitation has been thus aroused in large communities of negroes in southern Virginia, that it has been necessary for the owners of the land to compel the trick doctor to leave, for the tendency of this agitation is to disorder labor, as well as to disorganize the society of the race. There is no better proof of how high this excitement runs, and how supreme its influence over the mind and conduct of the individual is, than the fact that it is openly revealed to the whites. Of all their peculiarities of which they are aware, the negroes are most ashamed of their superstition, and yet it is so deeply implanted in their natures, and it has been so much fostered by their lives as freedmen, and their withdrawal from close contact with white people, that when it is inflamed by circumstances they cannot resist its promptings. They yield to these promptings with as much self-abandonment as to their religious emotions, and while in the power of the spell they will disclose their terror to white persons, to whom in moments of ordinary calmness they would be slow to acknowledge even that they believed in witchcraft, or, if they did so, would premise the confession with the statement that black people were subject to different natural laws from white, and that they should not be judged by the same rules. This superstition is generally kept profoundly secret from all save individuals of their own race. Having its origin in darkness it continues to lurk in darkness until one of those periods of agitation occurs, when every restraint is thrown off, owing to the force of the prevailing consternation ; each negro will then disclose with the ingenuousness of a passion the fear and anxiety that burden his heart and mind. There is something very strange and weird in the character of the negro's excitement under these circumstances. The unquestionable strength of his feeling, the sincerity, directness, and absoluteness of his faith, the vehement and tumultuous emotion that rocks his breast, the un- fathomable ignorance, the impenetrable darkness that envelops his intellect, all serve to sink what is merely ludicrous and laughable in his condition wholly out of sight and thought.

The negroes, however, do not believe that the power of casting a spell is confined to a trick doctor ; on the contrary they attribute this power to many individuals who are supposed to use the arts of witchcraft not for the purpose of earning a livelihood, but simply as a means of gratifying feelings of enmity. It is doubtful whether a violent contention ever arises between members of the race, that the party or parties on one side or the other are not convinced in the sequel that an evil charm has been laid on him or them, either through the intervention of a trick doctor, or directly by the malevolence of the person or persons engaged on the opposite side in the wrangle. This is very notable in the squabbles of the women, who are peculiarly bitter and rancorous when aroused. Overflowing with acrimony themselves, and conscious that they would not hesitate to employ any physical means of inflicting injury in their reach, they are always suspicious that their enemies have turned the black art against them in the same spirit that they them- selves have sought to turn that art against their enemies. No sudden death ever occurs in a community of blacks that is not ascribed by many, and in some instances by all, to witchcraft that has been brought to bear by some secret foe. A young girl in sound health is unaccount- ably attacked by a violent disease, and quickly dies ; the awed whisper passes around that she was tricked by an unfavored lover. A man in his hearty prime is stricken down, and passes swiftly away ; if he has recently been engaged in a quarrel, it will be said under the breath that this was the work of his adversary. The panic which such an incident will often create among them is indescribable ; a far deeper feeling being thus called into existence than a suspicion of poisoning would excite among the whites in any similar instance of a mysterious death among themselves. The art of witchcraft, the negroes argue, may be directed at any. moment against them, and from what quarter it will strike, in what manner, and at what time, they do not know, but this very uncertainty increases the terrors of their position by veiling its dangers.

It is strange that the sensitiveness of the race to anxiety and alarm on this score does not have the effect of discouraging altercations among its members. The fact that it does not shows how far they are swayed by transient emotions and passions, which they never check at the moment because then oblivious of every thing beside. They do not look forward to the possible consequences of yielding to such emotions and passions ; not seeming to anticipate at the instant that, in arousing anger in the breasts of the persons with whom they are contending, or even fighting, they may be laying up for themselves a store of future unhappiness through the application to themselves of those evil arts which their enemies can exercise directly, or through the agency of a trick doctor. Under certain circumstances, this fear of being tricked does exert a powerful influence on the conduct of many, whose real feeling would otherwise lead them in another direction ; as, for instance, in the case of a crime com-

mitted by one of the blacks against the whites. The
unwillingness of the great majority of the negroes who
are directly cognizant of such a crime, to aid zealously
and actively in the arrest of the felon, if left to their
own promptings, is due undoubtedly to the spirit of race,
which causes their sympathies to be fully enlisted on his
side ; but then there are many disposed to act differently,
who are prevented from doing so by apprehension lest
they may become the victims of witchcraft should they
dare to take a position in opposition to the mass of their
friends, companions, and acquaintances. Their lips in
many other situations are sealed where otherwise they
would speak out promptly and boldly, and their bearing
constrained where if they were removed from such influences their action would be wholly unreserved. As
it is, they are like men and women who have been placed
under a ban of secrecy and silence by an authority that
they can neither question nor resist.

There does not seem to be any form of superstition
among the blacks that resembles Myalism, except to the
extent of that peculiarity which has been mentioned as
belonging to it, namely, the association of witchcraft
with the healing art. But Myalism, in its broadest manifestations, is never exhibited. Although there are times
when a large circle of negroes believe that the spirit of
evil is abroad, let loose by the machination of those who
are full of hatred and vindictiveness towards their fellows,
yet no impulse is ever shown to exorcise this spirit by
resorting to a counteracting power. This was the
benigner element of the West Indian superstition. A
Myalist outbreak meant the repression of the malignant
influences of Obeah through the operation of a variety
of witchcraft inimical to it ; the atmosphere was tempor-

arily cleared by the destruction of all the work of the Obimen, and peace and good-will substituted for malice and confusion. A community of plantation negroes, on the other hand, seem to be ignorant of any means, on a great scale, of opposing the pervasive spirit of malevolent witchcraft. They stand in terror of each other, and though keenly frightened by the thought that they are surrounded by evil, yet have no scheme for removing it by a force commensurate with that which created it.

The faith of the negroes in witchcraft has increased since emancipation, as they have been entirely at liberty to follow their natural inclinations. Whenever they are free to follow such inclinations, the tendency of these is always to grow in vigor and intensity. Even when slaves, the blacks had their witch doctors, but the latter were careful to conceal their true character. At the present day a trick doctor openly pursues his profession, relying upon it for a livelihood ; he is only interfered with, and that comparatively rarely, by planters, who, impatient of the confusion that he creates among the negroes in their employment, threaten the law, or order him to depart from their estates. The general upshot of this is that he restricts his practice to the hours of darkness, at which time, if it is necessary, he can safely visit any plantation in his vicinity. The most probable danger now to be expected in connection with a trick doctor is that he will use drugs to consummate his predictions as to his influence over a selected victim. The poisoning of animals is growing to be a more common crime among the blacks as a means of revenge against such of their employers as have given them offense ; the poisoning of individuals, also, occurs for the same reason. To a certain extent, however, the faith which they have in witchcraft discourages the commission of this crime among themselves, for they consider a trick doctor fully competent to act as their agent in gratifying their vindictive feelings.

The increased importance of witchcraft has raised the dignity of the trick doctor, and he is not disposed to be over scrupulous either in impressing his dupes with his power or in satisfying their demands. Cases of poisoning have already been traced to this source, and there is ground for believing that the future will annually augment the number. How many really occur now, it is difficult to say, as the deaths of the negroes, however sudden or suspicious, rarely lead to investigation ; many die without the attendance of a physician, who might make a report, and thus the cause of their decease is only a matter of rumor. An impostor of this kind would not hesitate to commit any crime, if it could be done silently and furtively. In this, he resembles only too many of his race, who shrink from inflicting injuries openly and boldly, but are not loth to harm in an underhand way, as they are less likely thus to put their safety in jeopardy.[1]

[1] To show that the trick doctors are not confined to the remote rural districts, it may be mentioned that the number of Voodoo impostors practising their profession among the negroes of New Orleans—the tenth city in size in the Union and the second in the South—was found to be so great in the month of July, 1886, as to compel the Board of Health to interfere with a view to their suppression.

IX.

GENERAL CHARACTERISTICS—MORAL.

THE most remarkable feature of the general moral disposition of the blacks is the almost phenomenal development of the characteristics of the type as compared with the development of the characteristics of the mere individual; in other words, as members of one of the great families of mankind, they have the most pronounced traits as a race to distinguish them from all other races, but few peculiarities of their own as men to distinguish them sharply from each other. We can say this of them with far more truth than of any other people who have been brought under influences as varied and stringent as those to which they have been subjected. Their original spirit as a race has not been radically modified by transplantation to the American continent, the vigor and tenacity of their fundamental qualities having only grown more clearly perceptible with the progress of time, these fundamental qualities appearing to be incapable of alteration, however favorable circumstances may be to it. There are certain infirmities which characterize the race which, in this age at least, are as fully shared by the negro who has had every advantage of discipline and instruction as by one who has received no such training at all. Both are unable to resist the solicitations of their physical instincts, both are more or less superstitious, both live wholly in the

present, both show the same turbulent spirit when their
vanity is inflated, the same lack of fortitude in danger,
the same want of the power of concentrating their faculties in the form of continuous attention or resolution,
the same respect for unscrupulous force, the same abject
submissiveness when overawed, the same indifference to
suffering in animals, the same callousness associated
with amiability, the same harshness and tyranny when
in the possession of power, the same insensibility to
whatever is elevated in life and beautiful in the universe.
In short, we find precisely the same weaknesses in the
delegate who sits in the legislature, the teacher who
has been graduated from college, the preacher who has
studied the Bible, the house-servant who passes most
of his time in the society of respectable white people,
the land-owner who superintends his own hands, the
artisan who works in his own shop, the foreman who
holds the position of highest authority in the fields, the
common laborer who toils from morning until night
with his hoe or spade, the inhabitant of the pine
barrens who goes about in rags and can with difficulty keep from starving,—in all these, the qualities
of their race are so strongly and equally developed,
that the difference between the mechanic and the
teacher, the laborer and the legislator, is one of physical stature or shade in the color of their respective
skins rather than of natural temperament ; there is practically little if any difference in their moral dispositions.
The ditcher only lacks an equal amount of knowledge
to be as good an instructor as the teacher ; the plowman
would be just as competent a representative as the legislator.   Artisan and field-hand, land-owner and preacher
disclose similar characteristics as soon as they are

brought under the same influences ; and this is true of the blacks in every business and profession which they follow ; the force of identical circumstances develops in all the same traits which probably up to that time had been lying dormant. So equally, indeed, do they share the fundamental characteristics of their race, and so powerful are these characteristics, that it is not making too broad a statement to say that all negroes, with very few exceptions in proportion to the great mass, will act exactly in the same way in the same situation, and will display precisely the same qualities. If their situations are identical, then they are all as one person ; but if their situations differ, then they are unlike, too, to the extent of the difference in the influences of their respective situations. Indeed, whatever diversity of spirit is observed among the blacks is not so much in kind as in degree ; for instance, one is more ·genial than another, or more impulsive or more improvident, or more thoughtless, or more timid, or more sensual, but it is quite rare that a negro is distinguished for the opposite of any one of these qualities, even in a moderate state of development. They have the same underlying characteristics, but not to the same extent ; the root, if not the full flower of the same traits, however, is found in all. These traits are so vigorous and deep-seated, and, on the whole, so little receptive to influences that seem calculated to modify them, that the general disposition of the individual and the race can be studied with as much latitude and with as much thoroughness in a small as in a large community, or in one locality as in a whole commonwealth, or extensive region unconfined by State lines.

Slavery, by reducing the negroes to the same social condition, undoubtedly did much to dwarf the growth of distinctive individualities among them, but it did little to repress those moral qualities that belong to them as a people, if we except restlessness, for this it subdued with a firm and resolute hand. It is very plain that these peculiar qualities have been fostered much more under the new system than they were under the old, because every check that was put upon them then has been removed. The blacks are now at liberty to act just as they prefer to act, wholly unhampered by authority or uncurbed by public sentiment ; the unrestricted indulgence of their instincts in consequence, however injurious to themselves or destructive to society, has served only to fix these instincts more deeply in their natures. Then, too, emancipation enlarged the scope of these instincts, by increasing the opportunities for their gratification. When we compare the negroes who have come of age since the war with those who grew to maturity under the discipline of slavery, we find that the former are more impatient of every kind of restraint than the latter, and more eager and determined to escape from it. Their character approximates in other respects equally as important, more closely to the original African type than the character of their fathers who were once slaves. This is due partially to the fact that the whole race is fast reverting to the original physical type, and therefore to the original moral ; this is sufficient in itself to strengthen and intensify those qualities of the race that have always given it such a unique position among the various peoples who constitute mankind. The further development of these traits means the further departure of the negroes from the standards of the Anglo-Saxon. The new generation, in being less accustomed to restraint than the old, are therefore more inclined to act upon their natural impulses. They are more headstrong than their immediate ancestors, and to that degree, have a more decided tendency to retrograde. They seem to have inherited the unfortunate qualities of the slaves without having acquired any of the superior qualities of the whites ; the influences of freedom apparently failing to cultivate in them that respect for themselves which is the foundation of all that is excellent and admirable in character, and without which it is impossible for them to improve. They interpret liberty as signifying license only ; in consequence, they are not more correct in their conduct than the generation passing off the stage. Neither are they firmer and steadier ; they are rather more fickle and unstable. Nor are they more determined in maintaining their rights when these are infringed upon ; they are as easily overawed and intimidated. In short, we look in vain in the character of the new generation for those nascent qualities of a great people which the declining generation lack ; we find in them only too many of those qualities that have kept the African upon the lowest plane of humanity since the dawn of civilization.

When we analyze this general disposition of the blacks as a race, we find that it is especially remarkable for its inconsistencies. A few disconnected illustrations of this fact may he given. For instance, they show, under firm discipline, a degree of energy and a power of endurance that are unequalled by their sturdiest competitors drawn from the most resolute and industrious nationalities, and yet, as soon as this temporary supervision is relaxed, they will sink into habits of indifference and sloth that are only observed in the most enervated and effeminate peoples. They have the highest capacity for strenuous and continuous work, associated with the greatest proneness to indolence. When either of these opposing traits of the negro's individuality is exhibited, it seems impossible that the other can exist in such intimate connection with it that it is ready to disclose itself at any instant of time. Circumstances alone are required to repress the one for the moment and develop the other. Thus, laborers who will bustle forward in the sweltering harvest fields in cheerful unconsciousness of the heat to which they are completely exposed will be seen in the intervals of holiday strolling about with umbrellas carefully extended over their heads or lolling in the shadow of the eaves of the store. In the same spirit they will enter into engagements and perform, during the course of several months, the most exacting tasks with stoutness and alacrity, and then dissipate the rest of the year in puerile amusements.

Again, the negro may be anxious to acquire property, and yet it will not occur to him to repress those qualities in himself that obstruct the fulfilment of his wishes. He runs headlong into debt or wastes his wages in extravagant self-indulgence at the time that he is solicitous to purchase a tract of land or a horse, mule, or cow, or other form of property that will add to his permanent convenience and comfort. This disposition to neglect the means as adapted to the end in view is shown by him in all of his affairs and in every situation in which he is placed ; his indifference to the means, indeed, seems to be in proportion to his eagerness to secure an object, for this eagerness only makes him more heedless and impulsive. He would display the same carelessness whether acting for himself or merely as the agent of others in whose employment he may happen to be. The explanation of this lies in the fact that, however fully a wish or aspiration may appear to take possession of him, it is never vigorous enough to resist the force of some passing fancy or appetite, which may render its final attainment impossible.

A still more remarkable proof of the inconsistency of the general disposition of the negroes is that characteristic to which I have already alluded, namely, the intimate union of devoutness and immorality in their conduct. Those who are distinguished for the most sincere, fervent, and enthusiastic piety are often those who are most notable for violating precepts upon which the spirit of divine and human laws alike lays the strongest emphasis. They either do not recognize the relation of religion to their daily lives or they cannot but succumb to their impulses, however opposed to the lessons that they have received. To whatever level of vice or crime they may fall, they still retain and disclose the same religious aspirations, untouched by the least taint of hypocrisy and unobscured by the smallest shadow of doubt. These aspirations are entirely disconnected from their own careers ; being common to the murderers, ravishers, and thieves, as well as to those who, on the whole, are respectable men and reputable citizens, not resting upon any consciousness of depravity, but arising altogether unprompted and apart, being found as frequently associated with the grossest and most ruthless propensities as with mild and winning qualities.

Again, however amiable the negro may be, he is indifferent to suffering in the lower forms of animal life. There is nothing in mere helplessness that softens his sensibilities ; on the contrary, it is only sufficient for any living thing to be at his mercy for him to bear himself harshly or brutally towards it ; in this he shows a strong resemblance to children, although unlike children he is cruel, rather for the pleasure which the infliction of pain affords him than out of mere thoughtlessness. His cruelty, however, is generally free from vindictiveness. Even as a slave, when he was easily governed, he could not be prevented from maltreating the animals under his charge, and now that he is free he is more callous in this respect, as he does not fear his employer as much as he did his owner. His horses and oxen are commonly found maimed in a short time after coming under his control, the eyes of the oxen suffering especially on account of the heavy and sharp thong of the whip which he uses. He is often seen lashing his team without reason or provocation, while he sings with a cheerfulness and gayety that are not at all disturbed by the writhing of the unfortunate beasts. In the same spirit he takes delight in butchering beeves or mutton, although a mere apprentice, or in shooting curs that have been ordered to be killed. He will also cuff his children or speak to them more roughly than the occasion requires or his anger itself impels. The possession of power makes him tyrannical to its full extent, however jovial or light-hearted he may be, for beneath the surface of his character there is a certain bluntness and insensibility that circumstances can develop into reckless ferocity.

Again, although the negro is docile under strict and direct personal discipline, he is averse to restraint in his heart. As long, however, as he feels the pressure of a stern and exacting watchfulness, he yields to it with resignation and cheerfulness. He does not grow openly restive and turbulent even occasionally, but at the same time the desire to escape is not the less fixed and eager, as will be shown at the first opportunity.

In the same way, his submissiveness to personal authority is not accompanied by respect for the requirements of the general law when these conflict with his impulses, passions, or interests. The spirit of obedience which he displays when he is closely superintended causes him to do many things which he has no wish to do, or to refrain from doing many things he is anxious to do, whereas the fear of that legal punishment which he is assured will follow his acts does not prevent him from carrying out the intention of the moment, however improper or however criminal. The moral influence brought to bear upon him must be direct, resolute, and personal to control his conduct. No race responds more quickly or fully to such influences, or shows such insensibility to those that are impersonal and remote in a moral sense.

Another element of contradiction in the character of the negro is an alert imitativeness associated with the most wonderful persistency in conforming to the real bent of his nature. He is eager to ape the habits and customs of the whites, and yet reveals in his own infirmities that he is incapable of adopting any thing but the form. His disposition is constantly warping him from standards which he wishes to follow, and so far that aspirations that would otherwise make him more estimable only serve to disclose his weakness the more clearly, as these aspirations are so entirely out of sympathy and accord with his conduct.

These and similar inconsistencies that distinguish the race are not displayed by fits and starts like the contradictory qualities of mercurial temperaments that shift from one mood to another without any motive. However wide apart, and however unlike the points between which the pendulum of his individuality oscillates, the negro always acts in harmony with some feeling that overmasters him for the moment, and that feeling is the inevitable consequence of the fleeting circumstances that surround him. He is changeable only as these circumstances are changeable ; as long as they remain the same, he himself does not vary, but he responds at once to any alteration in them. He seems to be altogether incapable of bending circumstances to his own will, or rising superior to them by firmness of spirit. No one has more antagonistic qualities than he, but nevertheless of no one can it be predicted with more confidence and precision what he will do under the pressure of the same influences. He is hasty, thoughtless, and impulsive, and yet these characteristics do not force him to run counter to inclinations that his situation has raised. He obeys the natural voice within him wholly unconscious of those cross currents of feeling that so often perplex the wills of white men, or that spirit of self-repression that so often controls their conduct even when profoundly stirred ; the consequence is that all that is best in him, as well as all that is worst, finds outward expression in the most emphatic and energetic way, because in the most direct and untrammelled. One emotion succeeds another so rapidly in his breast when the circumstances brought to bear upon him are changing that it is difficult to recognize that he is the same person, so impossible does it seem that emotions so radically inimical, and disclosing themselves so diversely, can exist in the same person. These emotions are not superficial, but go to the very foundation of his character, and they deserve the warmest praise or the most severe reprobation as they touch either extreme ; and they are touching both so often that we praise and berate him almost in the same breath. He will expose himself to contempt one moment by yielding unreservedly to some depraved instinct, and secure respect the next by proving himself to be the most amiable of men, the most active of laborers, or the most obliging and cheerful of attendants. Here, for instance, is a domestic servant who happens to be inclined to petty thievishness. This subjects him to repeated rebukes, but if he is carefully watched and firmly managed, he does so well the work which he is ordered to do, he is so ready in performing any task which is given him outside of the province of his special duties, and is so faithful, on the whole, if he is not tempted, that his master will warmly declare that he is invaluable, nay indispensable, when perhaps the day before he was seriously turning over in his own mind whether he should not dismiss him. It is highly probable that the very man who would not shrink from filching his employer's property would rise with anxious alacrity at any hour of the night, however threatening the weather, if that employer were suddenly taken ill, would ride twenty miles if necessary through darkness and over rough country roads to summon a physician, would nurse the patient during his illness, and would hail his recovery with unaffected joy. Even more than that, the negro who, under the influence of a passing emotion of resentment for some trifling offense, would be the first to apply the torch to his employer's barn, or even to poison that employer himself, would perhaps be the very one who had during a long course of time served him with peculiar zeal and devotion.

It is one of the most notable peculiarities of the negro's character that it is not necessarily debased because it is

remarkable for criminal traits ; in other words, the fact
that he is wholly corrupt in some respects does not signify
that his general nature is demoralized. We often observe among the whites men who are worthy of esteem,
although addicted to certain vices, but never men entitled to it who are criminally depraved. When they
sink to the lowest point in one direction their entire
nature becomes degraded, because they recognize that
they have fallen irretrievably in the regard of their own
race, which reacts upon the opinion that they entertain
of themselves whether they are inclined to be shameless
or not. They see the public sentiment as to their conduct reflected in the glances of contempt, disgust, or
horror of their former friends and companions who
shrink away from them as branded with eternal disgrace.
Their own consciences convict them. They harden in
their wickedness under these influences, or their lives are
irrevocably blighted.

On the other hand, when a plantation negro is guilty
of crime, he is not made to feel the indignation and
scorn of his race ; he is received, on the contrary, as
cordially as if he had not committed an offense that
should properly fix an ineffaceable stigma upon his reputation. The faces of his associates are not turned away
from him, and there is no severity in their gaze. Then,
too, the sentiment of the white people with respect to
his act, however keen and bitter, does not affect him,
owing to the breadth and depth of the social gulf between them. The consequence is that no pressure of
importance is brought to bear to lower him in his own
opinion by degrading him in the opinion of others. In
the instance of some vices and crimes his character cannot be said to be demoralized, even to the extent of the

scandalous and profligate acts committed, because there
are some courses of conduct which the white people
consider to be abandoned and flagitious which the
negroes do not look upon as even immoral. When,
therefore, he falls into these, he does not experience a
sensation of impropriety or depravity. The corruption
usually attending them is not spread abroad through his
whole nature like a morbid contagion. Many of the
individuals of his race are eminently respectable as long
as they are not exposed to some form of temptation that
appeals directly to a special infirmity ; as soon as that
infirmity is touched, however, they show themselves to
be as corrupt to that degree as one who is unscrupulous
in all things. Those great weaknesses that we observe
in the characters of many white persons, associated with
the noblest and loftiest qualities, find their counterpart
in the individuality of the negro in vicious or criminal
traits, united to much that is worthy of affection and
esteem. In consequence of this singular inequality of
nature, there is, in some respects, less difference than
would have been expected between the disposition of
the average negro convict who is serving a term and the
average individual of the race at large. The divergence
between the dispositions of the two is rather in the comparative vigor of certain moral qualities, such as boldness,
resolution, and firmness, than in the groundwork of their
respective characters. The ordinary types of negroes
who are found inside of the prisons are not, as a rule, at
all unlike those outside, in the mere aspect of their
physiognomies ; occasionally a face is marked by deep
lines of brutality, or there is a sinister look in the eyes ;
usually, however, we discover in the countenances of the
chain-gang the same vacancy or amiability of expression

that we detect in the countenances of the members of their race whom we meet on the highways. When these prisoners are released and return to the neighborhoods where they formerly lived, they mingle as freely with their people as they ever did, and are not to be distinguished in any way from the mass.

Whoever seeks to judge the moral character of the negro without having any knowledge of him from personal contact, is very apt to be misled by the notion that he is merely a white man in disposition whom the Creator has endowed with a black skin. Plainly as his complexion distinguishes him from the whites, to the eye, it will be discovered, after association with him for a great length of time, to be one of the smallest points of difference between him and the Anglo-Saxon. Remove all trace of that color with which Nature has painted his rugged countenance, wash away every stain that darkens it, and the moral traits that seem to be peculiar to his race would cause him still to occupy an original and unique position. How far these traits will be modified in the future by the transmitted influences of a more refined and elevated condition remains to be seen. It may be true, as some ethnologists believe, that the highest personal type of civilization is far more a result of inherited instincts and knowledge than of innate superiority of race ; the future alone can verify the correctness of this theory in the instance of the negro. At his present stage of growth he resembles his former owner as little morally as he does physically. The two races undoubtedly share many qualities, because they have the same appetites which, working upon their characters in the same way, have left a similar impression. They are like each other to the extent that they belong

to the same animal kingdom, but there the likeness
ends.

The nearest approach which the blacks make to the
character of the whites, in traits not due to the influence
of their bodies, is to be found in their general resemblance to white children.   They have many of the
peculiarities of the latter owing to a common immaturity
of nature rather than to any substantial and permanent
similarity between the two races.   As a result of this
immaturity of nature, there are few essential differences
between a colored parent and his child except those that
belong to mere physical strength apart from the moral
disposition.   Father and mother, son and daughter,
however old the former and however young the latter,
are remarkable for the same inability to control themselves owing to common peculiarities of temper, for the
same dulness of the power of retrospection, and the
same lack of foresight.   Age seems to bring to the negro
no keener sense of the solemn mystery of life.   It gives
no breadth or depth to his character.   It breathes into
him little of that spirit which excites reverence and
veneration.   It invests him with little of that dignity
which ennobles gray hairs, feeble limbs, and wrinkled
faces.   The decrepitude of a frame that was once erect
and vigorous must always be impressive, but it is rather
as a general example of natural decay that he, bowed
down under the burden of many years, appeals to the
observer.   The fading of his various faculties is forgotten ; his dotage is pathetic only as a decline of his
physical powers.   The negro who has reached a mature
period of life bears himself with as much careless vacancy
of mind as if he had not passed his second decade ; the
same amusements afford him pleasure, and the same joys

enliven the passage of his hours that delighted him in his jovial adolescence. Time in its flight from day to day, season to season, and year to year, does not seem to touch him at all with that magical wand which works a far more wonderful change in the soul and heart of the white man than chemical forces do in material substances. As long as life itself lasts he retains the spirit of childhood. Youth does not altogether desert him ; its freshness, its inconsequence, its contentment with the present, its inability to look back on the past with regret or anticipate the future with fear, lurk in the recesses of his soul when his form has shrunk, when his hands tremble, and his feet totter as they walk.

The general impression after long and intimate contact with negroes is that, as a race, they bear the same moral relation to the Caucasian as a child does to an adult. It is just as if the race itself was an individual who had not passed that stage of growth which we designate as infancy. This immaturity, nevertheless, does not strike one as being such as the race, following a law as natural and inevitable as that which we observe in personal development, will necessarily outgrow. This may be due, however, to the mere effect upon the mind of discovering the same traits in the old and the young alike. When we compare the man of advanced years with the· youth, we detect such slight differences, other than those which are wholly physical, that to anticipate that the race will mature, in the light of that example, is apparently the same as expecting that a white man of powerful frame, but morally and intellectually blasted by disease very soon after his birth, will in time lose his deep-seated infirmities by the force of various influences. The immaturity of the negro seems at this period to be permanent, whether it is so or not. The impression which it leaves is both strange and startling, because we find it associated with so much corporal vigor. His moral deficiencies, therefore, instead of arousing our pity, excite a sensation of suspicion and fear. So much physical strength united to so much moral weakness is a combination of evil significance, although that weakness itself would be as unworthy of notice as the weakness of a child if he were as feeble in body as a child. He would hold a far more respectable position in the community in which he lives than he does now, if his infirmities were intellectual rather than moral ; he is stronger in mind than in character, and, in consequence, the part he plays is much more important than it is reputable. It is essential, therefore, that he should be educated more in an ethical than in a literary way, as a possible check upon those grave faults of character which the cultivation of his mental capacity would foster rather than remove. Before discussing the effect of the instruction which he has so far received in the public schools, it is proper that I should first dwell at some length on his intellectual, as sharply distinguished from his moral, disposition.

X.

GENERAL CHARACTERISTICS—MENTAL.

A CAREFUL observation of the intellectual character of negroes, creates the impression that their is a remarkable equality in their mental capacity, if we except a very few individuals. It is comparatively rare to find one who either rises above or sinks below the general level of the degree of intelligence with which the race is endowed. A transfusion of Caucasian blood, however, seems to quicken the African mind, and as the volume of that transfusion is increased, there is a nearer approach in many important particulars, to the intellectual traits of the white people. The mass of the mulattoes, however, although brighter and livelier in understanding than the blacks, are not, on the whole, distinguished for a notable superiority in mental grasp and comprehension. While the average mulatto pupil in the public schools, learns more readily and rapidly than his darker companions, and while too, a much larger number of scholars of his color may show proficiency as compared with the same number of young negroes of unmixed blood, yet the most intelligent representatives of the two respective shades, stand on the same footing, substantially, the pure black reaching this position of equality by greater toil and steadier plodding.

I shall omit the mulattoes from view, as a class that is likely in a few generations to revert almost wholly to the

original type in all rural districts where even now, they
are not numerous and influential enough to constitute
a circle of their own, which they can continue indefinitely
by intermarriage, and where, in fact, their rapid decline
in numbers, is due not only to the growing reserve of
the white men, but also to the marked preference which
the blacks themselves have for women of the lightest
complexion.

It is surprising to find that the negroes proper, rise
more frequently above the common level of intelligence
than fall below it. The exceptions to the general rule
are numerically greater in the former than in the latter
direction. In some respects, this common level is higher
than would have been thought probable ; it is questionable, indeed, whether there are any people who occupy so
low a position in the family of races, as observed in their
original habitations, and who have passed through so
much elsewhere that has been such as to continue them
in a degraded state, are superior within a certain range of
thought to the blacks, although that range is very narrow. Their mean condition, wherever found, is to be
attributed, in large measure, to their general poverty of
intellect, but it is due still more to the moral weakness of
their character, or rather, to certain mental weaknesses
that hover so closely on the borders of moral infirmities
that it is difficult to say whether they are mental or
moral. If their mental qualities were supported by certain moral qualities that have entered into the disposition
of every race that has attained to distinction in history
(and which has been considered a superior race principally because it had these moral qualities), then a notable difference would be detected in the vigor of their
intellectual powers, for these would not be dissipated or

hampered as they now are. One moral quality of this kind, which they lack, may be mentioned by way of example. This is what may be called, in the absence of a single term, continued or sustained force of will, in which the character of the negro is singularly defective, both because he is at the mercy of every transient emotion and passion, and because he has little capacity for concentrating his mental faculties, even apart from such influences. If the race were remarkable for unusual acuteness, the absence of this sustained force of will would obstruct for all useful purposes, the intellectual activity of its members. The general impression of intellectual weakness which association with them leaves upon the mind of any one who studies their peculiarities, is due more to the want of this faculty and faculties similiar to it, than to the inherent infirmities of their intellects, numerous and obvious as these infirmities are. The chief difficulty with which the negro has to contend in the practical affairs of life is not so much obtuseness, by which I mean confused perceptions that blind him to his true interests, as an inability, on account of certain moral qualities, to pursue uninterruptedly and without swerving, a course of conduct that is necessary to the accomplishment of his objects, at the very time that he clearly understands that such a course is necessary. It is owing to the absence of this sustained power of will, rather than to intellectual stupidity, that the negro stands so much in need of mental discipline to brace and strengthen his fluctuating and languishing intellectual energies. The advance that he has undoubtedly made, which is plain enough when we compare him as he is now, with his remote African ancestors, or with his contemporary kinsmen in the forests of the dark Continent, is due, in large measure, to that rigid supervision to which he had to submit as a slave, which enforced habits of application that were only another form of concentrated attention or fixed resolution. There can be no hope of the improvement of his race until this mental instability has been removed, and if this is impossible, then the race can never make any real progress beyond its present position. There is much danger, now, that the general laxness which enjoyment of freedom has fostered in its members, will destroy whatever impression the discipline of servitude left in this respect. Their present tendency is to revert to their ancestral condition in this direction, and this tendency will grow more pronounced, unless some substitute can be found for the discipline referred to. A purely literary education will not supply it. It is questionable whether any institution of learning could accomplish much for the overwhelming majority of the blacks, unless industrial or military training of a severe and exacting character was associated with the ordinary literary courses. That commonsense in which the negro is by no means lacking will not supply it. The fact that it does not, is palpable. He may comprehend very clearly what he ought to do for his own good, and yet his moral qualities are so overmastering that it amounts, in fact, to the same thing as if he were insensible to his own interests. This is very noticeable in the men and women who have grown up since the war, as compared with those in whom a spirit of self-restraint was more or less inculcated by slavery ; the consequence has been, that the former have not accumulated property in the same proportion to their number as the latter have done. The same trait, however, is found in both the older and younger generations, although in a different degree, simply because it is characteristic of the race. As a rule, the blacks are singularly aspiring, and yet how hollow and impotent this disposition appears, in most instances, not because it is unworthy and ignoble in itself, but because it is linked to moral qualities that make success practically impossible. It is rare even that it is invested with the dignity of an honest and strenuous effort to overcome the strength of these moral infirmities ; if it were, we would be moved at once to overlook every shortcoming. The negro is undoubtedly anxious to receive an education, and cheerfully undergoes many hardships to realize his wishes in this respect, but education represents a definite idea which his mind readily grasps. Here is the spelling-book, there is the slate ; the course is all laid out, the path is clear ; above all, he is under the constraining influence of his teacher, which is a direct and appreciable form of discipline. But if the object which he wishes to secure, is less tangible ; if to secure it, requires a constant and prolonged watch over his passions and inclinations ; and if he is supported by no strength except that which may lie in his own nature, then it is rare indeed that his recognition of what his true interests are, ever aids him to realize his aspirations. In short, he is as powerless for the want of sustained force of will, as a drifting ship without a rudder, because there is no quality in his character to take its place.

If the intellect of the negro is examined apart from the influence of his moral qualities, it will be seen to have a fund of mother wit and natural shrewdness ; in the larger sense, it is neither penetrative nor comprehensive, and yet within a limited field of activity, it has both keenness and grasp. His powers of apprehension are just and accurate in direct contact, although his conclusions are rather those of general intuition than a series of observations of even moderate exactness. No one, for instance, is more astute than he, in distinguishing the broader outlines of character of any person with whom he may be thrown in an inferior capacity ; he adapts himself with the ease and quickness of a lively discernment to all the leading peculiarities of such a person ; this facility and insight being partially due, no doubt, to the necessities of his position as a subordinate, which compel him to make a careful study of all the idiosyncrasies of his master or employer as involving his selfish interests so largely. So far as the general disposition of that master or employer is concerned, he is rarely mistaken in his opinion, his conduct in relation to such a superior, being but a reflection of the general qualities of the latter, although a mere inability to manage the servant or laborer is frequently to be attributed to previous inexperience of the character of the negro, or the application to him of the same standard by which white employès are judged.

The proverbs of the negro disclose a similar shrewdness, their range of observation being narrow and confined, but the observation itself, often acute. Above all, these proverbs are remarkable for their slyness and incisiveness of humor and force of good humored sarcasm. On the other hand, we discover in them no evidence of spiritual insight or elevation of thought and view ; and yet they are not lacking in poetic sensibility, especially when illustrated by metaphors suggested by the various forms of life to be found in the fields and forests. These metaphors, however, reveal only a superficial, casual, and transient glance. The truth is, that the perceptive faculty of the negro is very imperfect, but this is ascribable rather to his general carelessness, than to any real defect in this faculty itself which is incapable of a remedy. It is very inexact because he is deficient in his manner of contemplation, this being shown more particularly in his connection with the material world around him, both in its visible and invisible aspects. To a certain extent, he has an eye for the petty details of external nature, but he appears to be wholly obtuse to its larger and more subtle manifestations. Who lives nearer to Nature than he does? He has an opportunity of seeing every side of it as the seasons revolve, and as the months, days, and hours, succeed each other, in calm and storm, in sunshine and darkness, and yet he is scantily informed of its countless species of animal, insect, and vegetable life, and is strangely ignorant of its laws and the general spirit of its government. He shows like dulness, even when it exposes its beauties to his gaze in the most obtrusive way, as, for instance, in the glories of the morning and evening skies or the vernal and autumnal landscapes.

The best criterion of the perceptive powers of the negroes, with respect to what is visible in an ocular sense only, is their testimony in court. The most intelligent and conscientious white witnesses, to the same circumstances, often differ very much, as we know, in important items in their statements, but the blacks when put upon the stand very frequently diverge so much in their declarations as to the same incident, although they may have been witnesses from exactly the same point of view, that it assumes an opposite character as each one unfolds his story. This is due to no conscious design or even unconscious inclination to affirm what is not true ; their inaccuracy is a form of self-deception, not an intentional falsehood, unless their self-interests are involved.

It is a notable characteristic of the testimony of negroes that it always includes a great number of trivial and irrelevant details that they suppose to have been contemporary with the main incident in issue, their recollection of that incident being associated with many smaller incidents that have no real connection with it. In such testimony, too, one of their most conspicuous traits is very often displayed, namely, a certain mental exuberance that finds expression in an unmeaning verbosity. Their narratives, as a rule, are discursive, circuitous, and incoherent ; however simple and easy it is, apparently, to describe what they are called upon to do, their ideas, as they state them, are almost lost in the confusion of words. It seems to be impossible for them to be circumspect and even moderately concise ; interruption only deepens still further the maze in which they are toiling. It is not uncommon, however, to find among them an individual who is a fair reciter of tales, for in relating them he has ample room for the working of his power of imagination.

Within certain well-defined boundaries the negro is both prompt and adroit in putting forward such mental resources as he has. He shows this not only when he is suddenly placed in a situation of general danger from which he can only extricate himself by his wits, but also when he is charged unexpectedly with theft or other misdemeanor. The ease and gravity with which he will offer a plausible defense, or explain why it is impossible that he could have been guilty of the act, although in reality he was, are often inimitable. Even when confronted with incontestable proof of his offense, he will not infrequently shift his position and proffer a new plea without disclosing any trace of discomposure. While he displays this constructive power in a narrow sphere of thought, it never assumes the highest form of ingenuity ; he not only seems to be incapable of originating new ideas himself, but also of utilizing the ideas of others for new purposes. A notable characteristic in the same line is the little use which he makes both of his individual and the common recollections. While his memory is retentive of details to a certain extent, yet it never produces that general intellectual effect which is termed experience ; in other words, he does not seem to have any faculty that, seizing upon the mass of facts which his memory has stored up, either as belonging to his own past or derived from observation of men, the earth, and life in general, sifts and compares them, and thus obtains a countless number of deductions to regulate his course of conduct in the future. Experience with him is only a superficial mental impression which has no influence at all in governing his action. In fact, he dwells altogether on the present, except when he is occupied with religious meditations. Not looking behind or forward, he is unconscious both of the receding and the approaching shadows. Neither the past nor the future is taken into account by him. The consequence is that his insight into what comes immediately under his view, which alone interests him, is not clearer for what he has observed in the course of preceding years. It is impossible, too, for that insight to be just and accurate as long as he does not seek to anticipate the probable

relation of to-morrow to to-day. This mental characteristic was, no doubt, very much fostered by the influence
of slavery, which made it unnecessary for him to feel any
anxiety about his immediate future, as he was provided
for by his owner, but it does not wholly explain his
inability to utilize the past in the way of experience.
The want of this power is perhaps a corollary of one of
his most conspicuous mental deficiencies, namely, an
absence of logical force.   He has no turn for ratiocina-
tion, the temper of his mind being repelled by whatever
is intricate and complex.   His reasoning faculty is
subordinate to his imagination, which is the most influential of all the faculties of his mind, operating with
an ease and freedom that are not disclosed in the play of
the rest.   It is true that it does not take a lofty range,
even in exceptional flights, but this is due to his general
character.   It is exhibited, in its lowest phase, in the
whole bent of his superstition, in which it assumes the
grossest and most abject form of credulity.   On the
other hand, it is observed in the highest in a few poetical
proverbs, and in the mass of his folk-lore, which is
voluminous and detailed, reflecting both his humor and
pathos.   In this folk-lore the supreme importance of the
personal to the negro is again obvious ; his imagination
here does not impute original qualities to things, or
build up a separate system of its own, but merely
ascribes ordinary traits, aspirations, and motives in the
spirit of ancient fable.   There is some ingenuity but
little delicacy of fancy in its workings.   It deals with its
various subjects in a homely way, showing at every step
that peculiar tendency to moralize, that quickness in
detecting analogies, that element of rude common-sense
and shrewdness, to which allusion has already been made
as distinctive of the race.

When we pass out of this special domain we find that the imaginativeness of the negro is only that of mental immaturity. It is the exuberant and ill-regulated fancy of extreme youth ; it is but a singular intellectual fermentation that is uncontrolled because his powers of reason and discrimination are as weak as they are in children of a tender age. The man of ripe years has all the mental floridness of a boy whose faculties have not yet reached that stage of development when the imagination is submissive to the judgment, simply because the judgment, as yet, is lacking. As this imaginativeness is merely a characteristic of race immaturity, just as the imaginativeness of a child is but the characteristic of infancy (although this quality, as observed in the negro, is probably due somewhat to his tropical origin), it will pass away if he shall show that he is capable of moral and mental improvement under the pressure of the new influences. It has been predicted, in the light of this imaginativeness, that the negro is more likely to become distinguished in the future as a painter, poet, or orator than as a man of ability in practical affairs, but the probability is that, if it is possible to bring the race to maturity—a very doubtful hypothesis,—it will produce as many men of practical as of artistic talent, because the elevation of the negro will destroy his imaginativeness by removing his immaturity. His only chance of mental as well as moral elevation lies in the possibility that a race is able, by the force of favorable circumstances, to follow the same law of growth that an individual of a superior nature does. If this is so, his imaginativeness will be the first of his unfortunate qualities to disappear ; at present it is like a cloud, enveloping, confusing, and distorting the functions of his mind.

One of the most conspicuous results of this immaturity is that the negro has no grasp upon abstract ideas ; such 'ideas, however broad and generalized, find no lodgment in his brain. Whenever a subject is presented to him that has an abstract element, the latter is unconsciously ignored as being unintelligible. This is peculiarly the case in his religion. All terms that represent certain conditions of heart and spirit convey no meaning whatever to his mind ; and similarly with precepts that embody general rules of conduct, or brief expressions that sum up leading articles of faith. It is for this reason that the negro, while clearly understanding the mission of Christ, has no appreciation at all of those formulas of belief and behavior which He enunciated and upon which He acted.

On the other hand, the mind of the negro grasps with ease whatever is presented to it in a picturesque way. Many expressions in the harangues of his preachers and political orators have the same effect upon his mental sensibilities as a highly stimulating dram. There are certain ideas that throw him into a state of uncontrollable excitement. The sensuousness of his nature, in fact, is reflected as fully in the character of his intellect as in the temper of his body. There is, for instance, a very close sympathy between his mind and mere sound. It is observed that he is very much disposed to sing whenever he is engaged in performing an arduous task, as if he finds a subtle pleasure in the echo of his own voice, which sustains and invigorates his energies, however exacting the strain upon his physical strength and endurance. Any continuous sound, from whatever it may proceed, seems to exert the same influence ; thus, the hand shelling corn cannot refrain from joining in with the harsh roll of the instrument that he is manipulating, and the louder grows the noise which it makes the more fervent and resonant are the tones of his chant ; and so with the laborers who are standing near a wheat-thresher, the revolving wheel of which is filling the air with its murmur. In the same way the notes of a musical instrument, however rude, cause all of the negroes in earshot to strike their feet against the floor or ground, or to beat their hands together.

This sensuousness of intellect, united to great mental excitability, is revealed under a variety of circumstances, and of the general characteristics of the race it is in this connection one of the most peculiar and distinctive. It cannot be ascribed to that immaturity which causes the blacks to resemble children in so many of their moral and mental traits. It is rather a turn of disposition that is indigenous to a tropical people, being as much a fundamental part of the race as the pigments of its skin. It is largely due to this sensuousness and excitability that the negro is still an alien, although so many generations have passed away since he was transplanted to the American continent and brought under influences that were calculated to modify his original nature. These two qualities have done much to prevent him from taking a respectable position in history, and they are so deeply ingrained that it is doubtful whether there are any means in reach that would be likely to remove or even repress them. His mental excitability especially has been a stumbling-block in the path of his progress, for it is principally from this trait that his impulsiveness springs, which so often leads him to overlook what is plainly to his own interest. Above all, it is the source of his vanity which, upon the slightest provocation, assumes so many absurd or dangerous forms ; this vanity being a species of intemperance that permeates his whole nature, suppressing in him, when at its height, all thought except with respect to his own importance. It is peculiarly conspicuous in individuals of the race who have reached positions of comparative prominence, either in a political or educational way ;—authority, responsibility, supposed intellectual attainments, so far from sobering them, seem to turn their heads, although they generally maintain a grave and dignified bearing. The possession of power makes them harsh, cruel, and intolerant, not continuously and systematically, but capriciously, abruptly, and impulsively, while their consciousness of mental culture, so far from acting as an incentive, rather increases the vigor and intensity of their egotism.

The deficiency of the negro in original capacity is revealed in his total lack of any turn for speculation. His mind is never quickened and invigorated by scepticism ; he seems to have no desire to penetrate beyond what is merely visible ; the outer surface obstructs his mental as well as his ocular vision. His intellect falls at once into confusion as soon as it reaches a certain point, or perhaps it would be more correct to say that it seems to meet with a barrier in its effort to advance, which it cannot scale. It is owing to this restriction of thought, accompanied by certain grovelling instincts, that the system of faith that distinguishes the race wherever it has not been brought under the influence of Christianity is essentially bald, having no element of poetry in any of its various phases. This inability to break through the wall that encloses him seems to increase as the negro grows older. The precocity of the child is remarkable.

Its mind is quick, alert, and bright, but these qualities are very much modified at the age of puberty. That period at which the intellect of individuals belonging to other races grows stronger, firmer, and more comprehensive, is distinguished in the instance of such a child by a comparative arrest of intellectual progress. The advance after that is not at all in proportion to what had been observed to take place previous to it. The mind now becomes sluggish, narrow, and obtuse in many respects, just as if the development of the physical frame absorbed what should go to the support and enlargement of the brain. It is possible that this characteristic of the negro is due to the fact that he belongs to one of the tropical races, the individuals of which always ripen both mentally and physically much earlier than the inhabitants of temperate zones. The original law of growth peculiar to the race has not, perhaps, been modified in the American descendants of African ancestors, although these descendants have become accustomed to a different climate and condition. This cloudiness, which sets in at the age of puberty, is not removed by the force of experience in after life ; although the negro of advanced years has passed through vicissitudes that have in turn inspired him with grief, sorrow, pain, and anger, yet the perceptions of his mind remain essentially as they were before. His vision is not more unerring on account of his age, nor is his glance more penetrative. Indeed, however old he may grow, experience rarely irradiates his past with its light, or dispels even for a little way the shadows that darken his future.

Lunatics constitute a very small proportion of the whole population of the negroes. The causes of their mental aberration are generally wholly physical, the number of blacks who lose their wits for purely moral reasons being very insignificant, as might have been expected, both because the great mass are laborers who are kept very closely occupied, and because they are incapable of experiencing a great mental strain, except in the form of fear ; and it is only under the influence of superstition that they can be said to suffer from fear even for a sufficient length of time for it to have a weakening effect upon their minds. That severe stress, arising from settled grief or prolonged anxiety, which so often disturbs the intellects of the whites is unknown to them. They are naturally light hearted and easy tempered, and, therefore, even when they become agitated, the emotion is soon thrown off, however violent while it lasts. Idiocy, however, is as often observed among them as among the whites.

As a corollary of their comparative immunity from insanity for moral reasons, it is found that the blacks rarely commit suicide, a fact that is easy of explanation when a full knowledge of the character of the race has been obtained. In the first place, no cause of anxiety presses long enough upon the mind of the individual negro to foster a desire to put an end to life, this being another form of his inability to retain any one thought long enough to influence his conduct permanently ; then, too, he lacks the coolness and fortitude to destroy himself ; above all, he has a peculiar horror of death, owing to his morbid imagination, and not improbably to his tendency to live wholly in the present. His nature is impulsive and changeable. All his mental excitements, however extreme or uncontrolled, love, hatred, despair, sweep through the caverns of his brain like gusts of wind, and almost in a moment are gone ; hope happiness, and serenity soon return, and.he thinks and acts as if such transient experiences had never been felt by him, much less had left a lasting impression.

In all these general phases of his mental disposition, we discover again that likeness to a child that confronts us at every stage of our inquiry, and at every point of our examination. It becomes a question of extreme interest to find out how far education has modified the characteristics of the race, and what are the prospects, through its agency, of elevating its individuals to a higher position than they have hitherto occupied.

XI.

REMARKS ON PUBLIC SCHOOL SYSTEM.

PERHAPS it is too early to form a just notion of the part that the public school system will play in the future history of the negro. That system, however, has been established long enough to enable us to draw more or less accurate conclusions as to the work that it is doing for his benefit, and upon this basis some idea may probably be obtained of the relation which that system will bear to the general destinies of the race. There can be no doubt that the operation of the colored schools is attended with a considerable number of practical advantages,—whether any impression is made on the moral disposition of the pupils or not. These advantages are palpable and common-place. To have been taught to read and write with respectable skill does not signify a corresponding enlightenment of conscience, but it does mean an increased capacity for self-protection, and to that extent is unquestionably valuable. While the elementary knowledge imparted to the young negro in these schools is imperfect and defective—as a rule not enabling him to read the text of an ordinary book at a glance, or to write a series of grammatical and correctly spelled sentences—still it is thorough enough to be useful to him on the whole. An ability to read certainly assists him in getting a more exact idea of the agreements into which he enters, and an ability to sign his own name as one of the contracting parties would seem likely to invest these agreements with some sacredness in his eyes. This has been found to be the case in some instances, but it is generally admitted that the individuals who have been trained in the public schools are not more reliable in adhering to their engagements than those who belong to preceding generations. Unfortunately much of the rudimentary scholarship thus acquired—whether comparatively thorough in the beginning or not—is lost by the former pupil in the years that follow his withdrawal. He becomes a laborer or mechanic at once, and therefore has little time for reading after the work of the day is over, even if he feels the inclination—which he does not—and has books at his disposal. But he has no books ; there is not even a Bible in his cabin, and he never has an opportunity of perusing a newspaper. Year by year elapses without his refreshing his learning, and in time the principal part of it is obliterated from his memory— just as a fair acquaintance with the ancient languages is finally lost even by educated men after they become absorbed in the affairs of active life, although they may remember the meaning of many words or be able to translate a few sentences. His ability to write, however, serves, in some measure, to prolong his knowledge of reading, for the young negro is inclined to address an occasional letter to his absent friends. The information that he obtains of simple arithmetical calculation in the school-house perhaps lingers with him permanently, because it is brought into more use, being frequently of benefit to his interests. Thus it may prevent him from being cheated by his debtors and creditors alike. In assisting him to understand the casting of his accounts by others with clearness, it removes the suspicion on his

part of unfair dealing ; and it also helps him to keep his
own affairs in proper condition—probably cultivating,
to some degree, a spirit of ordinary caution and prudence in all of his pecuniary transactions.   The only
other distinct study included in the elementary course of
the schools is of no value to him in the management of
his private business.   The limitation of that course to
primary branches is eminently wise, and care should be
taken that this course should not extend beyond such
branches.   All endeavor in connection with it should be
directed towards making the knowledge imparted as
thorough and accurate as it is possible to be made.

Even if the elementary knowledge which the negroes
acquire in the public schools were useless to them in
after life, either because they are imperfectly grounded
or because what they learned there escapes from their
memories, yet there is one aspect of their education that
may partially justify the expense which it entails upon
the state, namely, the physical restraint which it enforces
for the time being, which would seem likely to be beneficial to all of the pupils.   They might in a few years
become oblivious of every thing that they were taught,
and yet a profitable influence resulting from this temporary restraint may remain.   In other words, if education
is not advantageous to them in a literary sense, it may be
useful to them as a series of tasks, both at the time that
it is given and afterwards.   They are inherently a restless and impulsive people.   Now that the strict supervision of slavery has been withdrawn they are left to act
upon their natural instincts, which tend to marked relaxation and to general license.   The true object of their
education should be to curb these instincts by the employment of every practicable means.   The mere fact

that the student is compelled, under the fear of punishment, to perform certain duties, whether he comprehends their purpose or not, is perhaps promotive of this end. Forcing him to concentrate his faculties for a special intellectual attainment is in itself a form of discipline. It is the spirit of the training that is desirable, rather than the nature or amount of what is learned. In this light the work of the school system in its relation to the young negro is probably valuable as far as it goes ; but it would be equally as valuable in this sense if that system only required him to come to the school-house at a stated hour every day and afterwards attend to certain tasks of a miscellaneous character, or if it forced him to chop so much wood or cultivate so much land.

Unfortunately, the young negroes who have enjoyed the advantages of the public schools are not remarkable for moral steadiness and sobriety ; the restrictions to which they have to submit in the school-house, seeming rather to increase their licentiousness as soon as they secure the right to govern their own conduct, as if the reaction carried them further than they would otherwise have gone. They are unusually restless as laborers and unreliable as individuals. In consequence of their lack of self-control and their unsettled habits, they have not accumulated property in the same proportion to their numbers as the freedmen have done ;—and above all, they show a disposition to adopt the lightest employments and to shirk all forms of exertion that compel them to put forth the highest energy. While these tendencies of the younger generation seem to disprove that the public schools foster a better spirit, the difficulty lies more in the character of the personal material upon which these schools have to work than in the character of the schools

themselves. They have to contend with the same obstacle that confronts every large institution in which only
literary instruction is sought to be imparted to the negro ;
the training of such institutions having been shown in
every instance, to be worthless in improving the material
prospects of their graduates, unless they become teachers, because the effect upon them, of a considerable
degree of literary culture is to put them out of conceit
with their sphere in life without strengthening their
faculties enough to enable them to rise to a sphere that
is higher. The course of the public school of the
country district, is extended enough to raise the ambition
of the pupils, but at the same time, it is barely probable
that it can ever leave such a general impression of moral
discipline as to make them careful and prudent in all the
practical affairs of life.   In fact, there is no substantial
ground for believing that the public school system will
have an important influence upon the material condition
of the negroes until it has been assimilated, as closely as
possible, to that type of normal school in which there is
a union of manual with intellectual training, the object
of the industrial education being rather to supplement
and enforce the mental, than to teach a special calling.
It would not, in fact, be well to overstock the various
trades.   There is but a limited room for mechanics and
artisans in rural districts at present ; the great body of
the pupils in attendance on the public schools can only
find employment as tillers of the soil, and therefore, skill
in handiwork will be of no real value to them.   An industrial element in their education, however, would not
only assist in cultivating a spirit of steadiness, but it
would probably have the effect of raising the dignity of
manual labor in their eyes.   It has been found that the

primary education which they receive in the public schools has a tendency to cause very many to look down on all forms of such labor with contempt ; an industrial training would counteract to a considerable degree, this unfortunate disposition, if stress were laid on it as of equal importance with mental training, or if it were brought forward as even of higher importance. Several objections can be urged against the introduction of such an element into the public school system ; thus for instance, it may be said, and with sound reason, that to maintain that system even in its present condition, and with its present purposes, demands a heavy rate of taxation. The first aim should be to perfect it upon the same line of operation, before its working is sought to be complicated in a way that will lead to greater expense. Admitting this, and admitting also, that an elementary education will to some degree, be useful to the negro, apart from the benefit of the moral and mental training which may attend the acquisition of a small amount of knowledge, it does not follow the less that the great object of the public schools should be to cultivate sobriety and industry in the pupils, and it is of no fundamental importance how this spirit is raised, provided that it is made permanent. Industrial training is entirely in accord with the only career open to the mass of the blacks. Such an education has been found almost essential even in the higher schools for the preparation of colored teachers, because it has brought the most powerful influence to bear to foster in them the spirit of discipline. I believe that the future will show that no training short of that which is considered to be necessary in the normal institute that educates its students with a special literary and industrial object in view, will be of lasting benefit to the negroes in the public schools, as far as these schools are supposed to equip their pupils for making their way in life. It will be further shown by the future that the public schools will advance in usefulness in proportion as they approximate to the system of a normal and industrial institute, and their failure to improve the material condition of the blacks, will be measured by their departure from this standard, or by their inability to approach it. What the young negro should learn, are lessons that inculcate repression of self as well as submissiveness to legitimate authority, and steady physical application; it is impossible to teach him these lessons by word of mouth, because he is, by nature, a creature of impulse, and therefore, a victim of his own restless, changeable, and thoughtless disposition. These lessons can only be imparted to him even temporarily by the exercise of an authority great enough to control and shape his actions. Unless the public schools can in some practical way cultivate this spirit of sobriety and these habits of labor, they will accomplish nothing towards the material elevation of the negro. If they do not fit him, either by direct training, or by general influence, for the battles of life, then their practical usefulness will not be appreciable.

As organized at present, and it is difficult to see how it is possible to organize it differently under the special circumstances, the public school system will not, in my judgment, work a substantial improvement in the moral condition of the negroes, by which I mean an improvement in their sentiment and conduct as men and citizens in all of the relations of life. In other words, it will not elevate the general tone of their society. Education has never had so many moral obstacles to surmount as in

a teeming community of blacks ; it may succeed in imparting to them knowledge, and not succeed in teaching
them morality, owing to that spirit which prevails among
the masses of the race in opposition to moral reformation.
This spirit is singularly hard to combat. The negroes
are receptive, sympathetic, and plastic, but these qualities are much more responsive to influences that emanate
from their own society than to influences that emanate
from any other source. That impression which negroes,
when crowded together, make on each other, which does
so much to destroy the force of ordinary religious
instruction, has a tendency to keep them in the same low
and degraded state, because it is powerful enough to
exclude or obliterate all other impressions. In a large
community of the race the principal influences are at
work to encourage what is evil and to repress what is
good. How indifferent the tone of such a community is
to what is wholesome and ennobling, is seen in the fact
that it is not at all modified by the best public sentiment
prevailing among the white people ; the character and
the scope of this public sentiment may be clearly recognized, and yet the negroes will either ignore it in their
personal intercourse, or they will openly deny its
applicability to their own society. No people have more
strongly-marked qualities than they have, even when
brought under a pressure that seems calculated to change
these qualities in the most fundamental way. Association with each other only tends to strengthen these
qualities, and in consequence of this fact, every
considerable community of negroes stands apart to itself,
being controlled by influences that arise in it, and being
little affected by influences that spring from without.
These internal influences unfortunately are not such as to

support the public school in the effort to elevate the general condition of the blacks ; on the contrary, the society of such a community is only too often distinguished for all those characteristics that have made it impossible for missionaries elsewhere to work any reform in the race, these characteristics, however vicious, being disclosed with all the freedom and unconsciousness of nature.

When we pass from the community to the individual child we find equal ground for discouragement, if for no other reason, because it is in the midst of such influences as these that the first impressions are made on his dawning and expanding intelligence, so soon to be the soil in which the teacher is to sow the seed of elementary knowledge. In that susceptible period when the germs of future goodness and excellence should be planted in the mind of the child, when his mother should teach him, at her knee lessons of veracity, honesty, and self control ; when his father should instil into him, the spirit of courage, manliness and strength,—how is he being prepared morally for the literary instruction of the school ? It may be said of him, as with too much truth of the older members of his family, unfortunately for them all, that his self indulgence is only restricted by his physical capacity and his opportunities. The discipline that his parents seek to maintain over him is alternately loose and severe, fluctuating without just cause from the one extreme to the other, and often lax when it should be harsh, and harsh when it should be lax. That discipline when it is carried to the point of punishment, is not attended by those gentle exhortations that alone make chastisement reasonable and just. It too often assumes the worse form, of unscrupulous power and brutal tyranny, being exercised rather for the temporary convenience of the parents than the permanent good of their offspring. In reality, no one instructs the child in those moral principles that he ought to learn before he enters school ; the darkness of his moral ignorance is not lessened, in anticipation of the literary training that he is to receive ; practically, the child, in that period which precedes his instruction by the public teacher, is entirely abandoned to the influence of his own instincts, unmodified by the simplest moral training.

Even apart from the working of all these hostile influences, whether they emanate from the community at large, the immediate circle in which he moves, or his home, his native temper would present many obstacles to a teacher. He has those characteristics of youth that are common to the children of all races, in addition to certain traits that belong to the individuals of his race alone. His mind is perhaps quicker and brighter than is common, but these qualities are associated with less frankness and ingenuousness than are usual in the disposition of the young ; he is inclined to be secretive and sly, and to that extent his nature is less open to the influences of education ; he has the restlessness of ordinary childhood united to an unusually rash turn of mind ; he is more intoxicated by the fresh emotions of youth than the white child ; he is more inconsequent and careless ; impressions on his mind and heart are obliterated more rapidly ; he rebounds from the pressure of authority with a larger degree of reaction, and is more impulsive, changeable, and capricious. Water itself is not more instable. In a thousand and one ways he discloses his tropical origin ; as for instance, in his excitability, the suddenness of his transformations, the sunniness and gayety of his temper. The peculiar idiosyncrasies of his race are constantly revealed in his conduct, child as he is, and closely as he resembles other children in those traits that belong to his period of life, irrespective of blood, color, or locality.

Such is his character when he presents himself for the first time at the threshold of the public school that has been erected for the country-side in which he lives. For that school to have any influence upon his moral development, it must take the place of his parents ; but the task thus assumed would be one of the most difficult to accomplish that could be imagined, even if the only object of the school was to give an ethical and not a literary training. Here is a child, remarkable in the first instance, for certain vigorous traits and instincts that he has inherited from a long line of ancestors, who approach nearer to barbarism as the line ascends, until finally they are savages as wretched and debased as have ever existed —savages who were, in fact, as nearly allied to the beasts of the field as to any human type, and to a certain extent sunk even below animals, by their superstitious and cannibalistic customs. Here is a child born of a race, the individuals of which have been under the heel of stronger races from the earliest date in recorded history, and who in all the centuries that have elapsed since the first annals were written, have not essentially changed in those qualities that placed them at the mercy of the resolute and unscrupulous. Here is a child who has spent the most susceptive years of his life amid surroundings that are calculated to implant the spirit of evil in his nature, whether it was there before or not by inheritance ; a child who has not received a single ethical lesson from parent or friend to prepare his mind and heart for other forms of culture. The first thing that such a child re-

quires is obvious ; he should be taught the plainest and
simplest lessons in the fundamental laws of common
morality. At the very time that this need is greatest,
because the formative period of his life is fast passing
away, he obtains only lessons in elements of knowledge
that cultivate his mental without cultivating his moral
disposition. To instruct him in ethics merely, might
well tax the energies of the most maternal, benevolent,
and sagacious woman, or the wisest, most patient, and
most persevering man. In only too many instances he
is so irreclaimable in spite of docility, so unalterable in
spite of gentleness, as to render all efforts useless, however wisely directed or however earnestly and continuously sustained. Even if the public school was only bent
upon his moral improvement, there would be the same
influence to contend with that did so much, as has been
stated, to mould his character in the years that preceded
the hour when he was placed under the instruction of the
teacher, namely, the injurious influence which the society
in which he daily moves would exercise after school hours
in opposition to the nourishing influence of his teacher.
The colored pupil returns to a household that is far from
being careful in the observance of the ordinary proprie-
ties and decencies of life ; it is, in fact, only too often
wholly oblivious of all that is upright and beautiful in
any of the personal relations, as well as blind to every
obligation and indifferent to every responsibility. This
household is composed of his own flesh and blood—
father, mother, brother, and sister,—who naturally would
have much more control over him than the teacher, with
whom he is thrown only during a brief part of the day.
Even if the members of his family were very respectable,
he would probably be led astray by the example of the

young companions with whom most of his time would be spent, or by the spirit of the community in which he lives.

Now, the public school system does not seek to instruct the young negro in morals, its aim being to teach him the elements of literary knowledge only. The evils which an ethical education of the pupil would have to overcome, namely, those arising from his associations outside of the school-room, are present also in the instance of a mere secular training ; in fact, the influence of this intercourse is more powerful when literary instruction alone is given, because no effort is made in the school-room to combat it specially. As the scholar advances in the rudiments of knowledge he does not acquire the rudiments of morality, and, therefore, the process of learning is attended with serious danger to the pupil if carried beyond a certain point, where the cultivation of his intellectual faculties will only enlarge the scope of his uncultivated moral faculties. It has been observed in the higher institutions for negroes, that as they have made progress in mental culture, they have been inclined to think that the ordinary rules of propriety were not applicable to them. In their satisfaction with their attainments, they have been disposed to consider morality as of no importance. Their growth in character has not been in proportion to their growth in mind, and this too when they have been compelled to submit to the severest discipline, tempered by the most earnest regard for their welfare. In the public schools, in general, there can be no such discipline as this exercised, except in the hours of recitation, and then the attention of the pupil is absorbed in his ordinary studies. That moral improvement which many negroes show under close supervision, and which they rarely show under other circumstances, is not observed here, because the supervision is interrupted during the greater part of the day, when the pupil is brought under evil influences, that are more likely to impress him than such excellent influences as may emanate from the school itself.

Not until the public school for the blacks becomes as much a religious as a literary institution ; not until it is directed more to the ethical than to the mental training of the pupil ; not until it is bent rather upon the education of his instincts than the cultivation of his mental powers, is it likely to create in him the slightest inclination to resist the force of the evil conditions that surround him. It cannot be reiterated too often that the negro of the new generation should be trained, if possible, to be steady and sober, not only for his own sake, but for the sake of the community in which he lives. The object of the public school should be to teach him to control himself, and every possible means should be employed for that purpose. It is not enough that he should learn how to read and write ; it is far more important that he should be taught to be honest, temperate, and self-restrained. It is probable that these qualities will not be imparted to him to a considerable degree by any general system of education, but certainly not unless the religious element in his instruction predominates over all others. If there is no such element, then the true basis upon which every form of educational discipline should rest will be lacking. The first step necessary to be taken with a view to the introduction of this religious element is to supply them, without exception, with teachers who have passed the ordeal of normal institutes, in which more attention is paid to ethical than to intellectual training ; in which, in fact, the mental and manual education received is given with a view to the moral effect alone ; men, in short, who have been selected for their fitness for a special moral rather than a special intellectual task ; men who have been trained to be missionaries. To raise this spirit even in the most respectable negro is a grave and arduous undertaking, but if it is ever possible to do so in the highest degree, it must be in normal and industrial schools in which the character of the pupil is subjected to the most rigid discipline. If this spirit can be imparted to him he will go forth with a well-defined purpose to Christianize not only the children whom he instructs, but also their parents, crossing weapons with the preachers and politicians who use their powerful influence to increase that low sentiment among their people, on which they thrive. Probably the task is too great for the capacity of the negro, for it is a task demanding the most delicate tact and judgment. If, however, the increasing army of teachers were all graduates of normal institutes that first seek to nourish a true religious feeling in their students, there can be little doubt that the evils that now threaten every community in which the negroes predominate would be diminished. The obstacle in the way of the establishment of a large number of institutions of this kind is their great cost, but the tendency of any improvement in the public school system is towards their erection, for, as experience makes the system more useful by perfecting its methods, as public sentiment with respect to its objects grows more enlightened, the necessity of having such institutions will become more obvious as bearing directly on the moral and industrial future of the negroes, and through the negroes, upon the prosperity of the community in general.

XII.

THE NEGRO AS AN AGRICULTURAL LABORER.

In considering the negro as an agricultural laborer, we view him in that phase of his general life in which he appears in the most familiar light. The vast majority of those who till the soil and prepare the crops for market belong to his race ; and their number alone would invest them with remarkable interest, whether we regarded the character of their work or not. The great amount and inestimable value of that work raise them in the present age to a position of the highest economic importance. In every community in which they constitute even the smaller proportion of the inhabitants, they form the principal part of the laboring population, for the reason that all negroes, with very few exceptions, are included in this general class ; those individuals among them who follow a profession or mechanical trade sinking into insignificance amid the swarm of their people who earn their bread by various manual tasks.

There is no record of any agricultural laborer who excelled the negro as such when he was a slave. Docile, obedient, cheerful, unresentful, of remarkable strength and unusual powers of endurance, he lacked no quality which a tiller of the soil should have, except that it was more or less necessary that he should always be carefully overlooked ; but under such supervision, which compelled him within proper limits to put forth his highest physical capacity, he had few, if any, deficiencies. Apart from this supervision, he was inclined to allow both his attention and energy to relax ; but this might have been expected, as he was without any real incentive to work. This discipline to which he was rigidly subjected, left a deep and abiding impression on his character ; it cultivated in him a spirit of industry, which he disclosed at once as soon as he was properly directed ; and it lessened his native tendency to indolence, even when he was aware that he could be idle without risk of rebuke or punishment. Emancipation was followed by far less disorganization of labor than would have been anticipated, simply because those habits of industry which slavery had created came to the aid of the freedmen when they found that they had to work or starve. It is improbable, however, that these general habits would have stimulated them to exertion at all, if they could have secured a livelihood as easily as their fellows in the tropical islands of Hayti and Jamaica secured it ; but being forced by local circumstances to earn, by the sweat of their brows, the bread with which they supported life—a fate that was most fortunate for themselves as well as for the community in which they dwelt,—these habits of industry, which had been formed under conditions that had passed away forever, arose in good stead, to assist them in adjusting themselves to the new economic relations which they bore to their former masters, as well as to the land itself, which they had been cultivating for so many years as slaves.

The first effect of emancipation upon many individuals of the race was to inspire them with a desire to abandon the scenes that had been familiar to them as slaves, and they promptly acted upon this impulse ; separated from their former homes by their own determination, they obtained employment elsewhere—in many instances in distant parts, of which they had no previous knowledge. Some even doubted whether they had been really liberated until they had tested their ability to leave the old localities without opposition from their former owners. Even if they were confident that they could do so just then, they anticipated that their present liberty would be curtailed so much in the future that they would practically be reduced to their original condition again. An emotion of fear, therefore, urged them to depart. Fidelity, timidity, or sound judgment induced a few to remain permanently where they had always lived, but the vast majority of negroes changed their habitations either immediately or in the course of the first years after they were set free. Many of the largest plantations were almost depopulated of their former laborers, the places they vacated being filled by those who had immigrated from other sections or had come in from the same country-side.

At present, the laborers are not inclined to emigrate to a great distance by the mere force of a migratory instinct ; a few do so under the terms of temporary contracts into which they have been tempted to enter by the solicitations of agents, but a large number are rarely influenced to remove in a body to far off States in the mere hope of improving their condition. Within the circle of an extensive division of country, however, they are constantly shifting ; they will rent land for one year and set up on their own account as mechanics the next, or they will work for one planter a month and labor in the employment of another for twelve months, or attach themselves to the same plantation for many years, and then suddenly announce their intention to leave. The fact that the laborers of each community are changing so often, introduces an element of instability into their social life, which encourages immorality and a disregard of obligations among them, for when they desert one community for another, their connection with the first ceases in every way ; they are disposed to ignore their debts and not infrequently their marriages, too, if they leave their wives behind ; in other words, they start anew as if they were untrammeled, and their ability to do so, is a strong inducement to them to rid themselves of their burdens in one locality by settling in another at a distance.

This restlessness is the only ungovernable fault of most of the laborers who were trained under the strict and regular discipline of slavery. Apart from this unfortunate trait, which can be somewhat restrained by skilful management, the majority of the freedmen constitute a force of working men that cannot be surpassed in efficiency. Their submissiveness to authority still survives, and they still retain their habits of industry. On the whole, they are steady, docile and active ; but the display of these excellent qualities is, to a very great extent, dependent upon various conditions. In the first place, they appear to most advantage on extensive plantations, for there, they are happier and more contented, on account of the continual gratification which the society of so many individuals of their race affords them. Some of these plantations include several thousand acres in one body, and it requires many laborers to cultivate their soil. These with their families occupy the quarters in which the former slaves dwelt. Although they can obtain the permission of their employers to visit any part of the country, although they can rove as much and as

far as they like, after the work of the day is over, or on
the occasion of a holiday, the principal portion of their
lives during the period of their connection with a plantation, is spent there.   Each of these large plantations is
almost as distinct a community under the new system as
it was under the old, in spite of its being in much more
direct communication with the surrounding country than
it formerly was, and in spite of the frequent mutations in
its population. Its inhabitants, in an extreme emergency,
could supply themselves by their own skill and ingenuity,
with every thing that they now purchase from abroad,
and if withdrawn from all other society, the company of
each other would satisfy their love of companionship.

Such local influences as these unite to diminish the
restlessness of the freedmen by attaching them more
firmly to the soil ; and to that extent, these influences
lead them to be steady and industrious, as their minds
are not diverted or their energies relaxed by the constant
prospect of a change.   They are also incited to exert
themselves by having many associates as they perform
their tasks in the fields or manipulate the crops in the
barns ; an ability to converse and make merry as they
work, operating as a spur.

An uninterrupted superintendence, however, is necessary to their activity.   A gang of men who will labor
with the most cheerful and unremitting industry under
the eye of a firm and watchful overseer, without requiring a word from him to urge them on, will, if he withdraws, begin at once to lag, and it is not improbable that
in a half hour they will be leaning on their hoes while
they engage in lively conversation ; or, if they continue
to work, the effort will be irregular and languishing.[1]   It

[1] This is true of the laborers irrespective of age.

is one of the most remarkable of traits of the field hand, as of the house servant, that he does not openly rebel against the strictest supervision, although it is opposed to every instinct of his nature ; on the contrary, he responds to it as readily, apparently, as if he admitted its necessity, and was glad to be sustained against the impulses of his own weakness. It is absolutely essential, however, that the spirit of this supervision should not only be constant and resolute, but also just and thoughtful. If the employer or his overseer is harsh and indiscriminating in his discipline, taxing the energies of the freedman to a point that shows a lack of proper regard for him, the latter is disposed to resent it by leaving. The recognition of the quality of honesty in the character of the employer, the certainty that he will act with fairness in all the various transactions that may arise between them, a consistent adherence to his promises, prompt payment of whatever can be claimed as due,—all these things unite to make the negro, whether trained under the old or new system, more industrious and less unreliable as a laborer. And what is equally promotive of this end is an inclination on the part of the employer to favor his laborer whenever circumstances allow him to do so without affecting the proper management of the estate. Thus granting all reasonable privileges that will increase the comfort of the laborer, such as permitting him to fatten several hogs, to cultivate patches of ground, not only in vegetables but in corn, keeping him supplied with wood, advancing small amounts of money occasionally during the course of a holiday, or perhaps giving provisions when he celebrates an important entertainment. In short, there are many acts of kindness which the planter can do, within restricted limits, without injury to himself, that will go far to make his employés, whether old or young, contented, and thus increase their usefulness as laborers by repressing their love of change.

It is characteristic, however, even of the most respectable negroes, who were trained under the régime of slavery, that they will disregard a contract if it conflicts with their interest or caprice. They seem to be entirely oblivious of the binding force of an agreement, as if it had no well-defined meaning to their minds, not even when it is considered in the light of an ordinary promise that passes in conversation. In consequence of this indifference to a contract, there is no way whatever of retaining them if the plantation with which they are temporarily connected is situated near a convenient means of transportation, such as a railroad. Under these circumstances they often suddenly move to a distance, being led by mere impulse or the prospect of higher wages to abandon their present employer, without even informing him of their intention

The laborer who has grown up amid the influences that have prevailed in the society of the negroes since the late war, is inferior in steadiness, even under supervision, to the laborer who was once habituated to the restraints of slavery. This is not surprising when it is recalled that he has practically been his own master from the time of his childhood, not having been subjected to any rules of conduct that were likely to make an impression on his character. As he has never been systematically taught to submit to discipline, he is very much disposed to chafe against the authority of his employer, not in a rebellious spirit while it lasts, but with a desire to bring it to an end as restricting his independence ; and therefore he cannot be confidently relied upon to remain for any length of time in the service of any one person. He shows a hearty dislike of being bound down to one spot, even when he is aware that it is advantageous to his interests that he should be ; his feeling in this respect being so well known that the planter for whom he may be working, at any season of the year, is careful, as a rule, to refuse him credit unless he has a family, which hampers his general freedom of movement. His natural impulse is to earn his livelihood by light jobs that do not encroach much upon his time or tax his strength too heavily. If the exacting character of his situation only permitted it, he would not exert himself at all ; but it is absolutely essential that he should, to obtain the ordinary necessaries of life. He shirks the task which nature imposes just as far as nature itself will allow. He strives to ease the burden which it places on his shoulders, not only by following the least arduous employments, but also by wandering in a restless spirit from neighborhood to neighborhood and county to county, passing a month or two in one locality, perhaps, and moving quite rapidly, from point to point, during the remainder of the year. The planters complain that he is disposed to stay with them as long as the weather is cold and the country closed by frost, but that he will leave as soon as spring has fairly opened, when his services are indispensable.

As laborers, the members of the new generation are very inexpert in many important respects, because their employers cannot enforce the degree of discipline necessary to instruct them ; but even if their employers could do so, these young men rarely remain long enough under the supervision of any one planter to allow him sufficient time to teach them to the required extent. Thus, in all those counties of the tobacco region of Virginia, in which the crop is cultivated and prepared for market entirely by negroes, there has been a notable decline in the quality of the staple as well as in the character of its manipulation, now that the majority of the hands who were trained for many years under the eye of their master or his overseer, are fast dying off. This is a crop that demands unusually careful management to put it in the proper condition for sale, and any lack of skill or knowledge in those who have charge of it is plainly revealed in its final state, when it is exposed to the purchaser in the warehouse or on exchange. The deficiencies of the laborer in connection with this staple cannot be supplied by the prudence and watchfulness of the employer, as it is possible for him to do in the instance of the cultivation of such cereals as corn and wheat. Here much depends upon the preparation of the soil and its cleansing after the seed has sprung up above ground ; but the grain, when it has matured, needs no extended manipulation, Tobacco, on the other hand, requires the most thorough information and the most discriminating skill from the hour that the plant expands in the patch to the moment that the leaf is prized in the hogshead. Under the old system each plantation had its circle of slaves who were carefully educated from childhood to do general or special work, and the individuals of that circle attained to much expertness in the various tasks of the barns and fields ; but under the present system this is impossible, and the result is that the labor of the new régime is generally inferior in character.

This decline in the expertness of the negro as a laborer will undoubtedly affect his condition profoundly. It has already been injurious to his interests. Many instances can be mentioned of the greatness of the obstacle which his lack of care, foresight, and discernment places in the path of his material progress. One may be cited as a fair example of the rest. In certain parts of Southern Virginia, where the celebrated variety of tobacco known as yellow tobacco is produced, a plan for curing it in the barn has been adopted, which requires incessant alertness and watchfulness to prevent the dry leaf from being exposed to conditions of the atmosphere that would either injure or destroy it in a short time. To conduct the process of curing properly, demands not only experience, but also close attention and excellent judgment. It has been generally found that the negroes cannot be safely trusted with the exclusive supervision of the barns under these critical circumstances. Their minds are too apt to wander from the duty in hand ; they unwittingly forget to observe the thermometer with a view to keeping the temperature at the proper rate ; above all, they have a marked disposition to doze and sleep, and during the time of their drowsiness or slumber the fires in the barn either decline or grow into too fierce a flame. In fact, it may be said of all the laborers with much more truth than of the house servants, that they cannot be relied upon to perform any task, which would be either dangerous or fatal to themselves or to the interests of their employer, if they showed that they were lacking in vigilance, prudence, or self-possession. It is due, in some measure, to the increasing defects of the field hands, as well as to the difficulty of enforcing a strict authority over them, that there is a growing tendency towards the division of the great plantations into small plantations, that can be cultivated by the owners with the assistance of a few men who will be compelled to work under their immediate direction. Much more powerful influences than this are operating to break up the original system with its single estates, including many thousand acres, and its large gangs of laborers. The complete disruption of this system will have a very injurious, if not fatal, effect on the interests of the mass of negroes, as it will throw the tillage of the soil for the most part into the hands of white men, who are members of the proprietors' families. At the best, it will deprive the blacks of many opportunities of accumulating sums with which to purchase small tracts of land for themselves ; in most instances those who have laid by money enough to buy such tracts have been able to do so by their connection with the owners of large estates. The disruption of the system of great plantations will force the negroes back upon the barren, inaccessible, and sparsely-settled ridges.[1] Those who inhabit these ridges have always lived in a meaner way than the laborers who are employed in the low lands, because their ability to earn a livelihood is much more precarious. In consequence of their extreme narrowness of fortune the rate of mortality is much higher among them, their food being scantier and less nutritious, and the medical attendance which they receive when sick, if they receive any at all, being of an unskilled character. On the whole, however, the breaking up of the old plantation system has not yet reached such a point as to produce much alteration in the life of the laborers. The country is still held in tracts of considerable extent, not so much from any desire on the part of the proprietors to retain their land in this form,

[1] In the end the disruption of the system of large plantations will probably have the effect of excluding the masses of the negroes from the soil altogether.

as from their inability to sell it. As renting has been found to be unprofitable, the inclination of the planters in general is to cultivate their own soil, and to do so they are compelled to rely upon the mass of negroes for labor, the negroes in turn being forced by the spur of poverty to work, whether naturally disposed to do so or not. They may shift uneasily from one locality to another, and change their employers every year, or even every month, according to interest or caprice, but the constraint that they are under to earn a subsistence remains wherever they may be, and this necessity is advantageous to the country in which they dwell. If they could live without toil, and yet continue to increase, they would soon destroy the prospects of every community of which they formed the principal part.

The large planters prefer to make up their complement of hands by employing negroes alone. Long intercourse with the blacks in this character have accustomed their former owners to consider them only in the light of a population that is adapted by their physical qualities to the tasks of the fields. Tradition also has a powerful influence in producing this state of mind in the leading planters ; then, too, association has thoroughly familiarized them with the African temperament, which enables them to manage their colored laborers with comparative facility. But their preference in this respect is chiefly ascribable to the perfect contentment of the negroes under circumstances that excite in white laborers the profoundest dissatisfaction. The difference between the white and the black employés on the same plantation is very much in favor of the latter in the point of cheerfulness. While the negro will go to bed contentedly when he can see the sky through a hole in the

roof, and eat his dinner from a tin bucket when sitting
on a clod, the white laborer is captious and resentful,
complains of his wages, his quarters, and indeed of every
condition under which he lives.   Nearly all of the latter's serious faults as a laborer proceed from pride and
a desire for a better position, and all the merits of the
negro from a total absence of either.

It is observed that the white men who are employed on
plantations that are thickly inhabited by negroes are
always restless and uneasy if their duties bring them into
contact with the other race ; necessity may force them to
work side by side with the blacks in the fields, but in the
majority of instances, they will only do so as long as they
cannot avoid it.   The degradation of the association as
well as the meanness of their condition are not forgotten
for a moment, and it is highly probable that they will
break through their contracts before these have expired.
They do not show this disquietude if they are carpenters
or mechanics, or if their tasks do not compelled them to
be thrown with the blacks on a footing of equality.   It is
due to this feeling that white labor is slow to compete
directly, and in the same field, with negro labor.   In a
certain sense, the abolition of slavery emancipated the
lower white classes as much as it did the black, for there
can be no doubt that it raised the dignity of manual
work—but prejudices of race still survive. We see as
strong an inclination in the two peoples to separate in
the tobacco lot as in the various walks of society ; a
common poverty and a common necessity to win bread,
it would be supposed, would break down the barriers of
sentiment in the fields and barns, but it does not.   This
sentiment is not observed where the land is held in small
tracts that are cultivated by their white owners with the

assistance of a few negroes ; whites and blacks here toil together in the closest contact, but their relation is not one of equality, as they do not meet as the laborers of one proprietor, but as employers and employés.

It is plain that in the general conflict between whites and blacks as laborers, the negro enjoys the chief advantages. He is physically as vigorous and stanch as the white man ; and is more cheerful and more easily managed ; he lives in happiness under material conditions that would be intolerable to the humblest white laborer : and has no sentiment or pride that will prevent him from seeking any kind of employment, however disagreeable that employment may be to ordinary sensibilities, or in what degraded situations, it may place him.

Not only can the negro successfully compete with the native white man, and drive him from the field, but he is also able to expel the immigrant competitor who does not shrink at all from working in his company and at the same tasks. The immigrant laborer does not strive long to rival him, because no such laborer is content to live on the same humble plane of existence ; in this, the latter resembles the native white laborer, only that he is far more irritable and complaining. He is dissatisfied even when he occupies a position in which a native white man is entirely contented ; and when he is ordered to do the lowest kinds of duties his objection is so strong, that he soon brings his service to an end. The same amount of wages on which the negro can subsist with ease would not procure for the immigrant workingman what he considers to be the barest necessaries of life ; his dwelling would be a log cabin, or perhaps a shanty ; his food would be of the plainest and coarsest nature and his clothing of the rudest texture. These conditions combine to discourage him from competing with the negro, and to that extent, the latter exercises a most injurious influence on the fortunes of the country in which he lives, even in that character, in which he is entitled to respect, namely, the character of a laborer, for in obstructing the immigration of foreign workingmen, and in throwing a shadow over the prospects of the native white, he really excludes foreign capitalists[1] from the community to a very considerable degree. It has been observed that the immigrant land-owners, having never been brought into contact with negroes before, find it impossible to harmonize with them. Accustomed to white laborers, who require no continued supervision to compel them to perform the tasks that they have agreed to perform, these proprietors are harassed by the uninterrupted necessity of having to look after their colored employés even in the smallest details, and under circumstances, in which it would be supposed, habit, experience, and observation, extending over many years, would have trained the employés to the highest efficiency, without personal direction. The immigrant proprietors find themselves contending without intermission, with the natural indifference, carelessness, and supineness of the black laborer. Their tempers, in consequence, become exasperated, and they are apt to be strict and uncompromising, without any leaven of kindness. Against this, the nature of the negro rebels, his indifference and carelessness increase, his energies decline, he is ill at ease, and wholly out of accord with his situation.

The native proprietor, on the other hand, who has

---

[1] In the terms "foreign workingmen" and "foreign capitalists," I include workingmen and capitalists from the States that were known as the Free States before the emancipation of the slaves.

been accustomed to colored laborers alone, has been taught by long experience that they can only be controlled by a judicious mixture of sternness and leniency ; that many weaknesses and deficiencies in their character have to be overlooked as incapable of a remedy, and that a proper allowance should be made for these faults and their ill effect removed by constant watchfulness and care. There can be no doubt, too, that these weaknesses in the negro laborer foster, in some measure, the same weaknesses in the native proprietor himself. He becomes infected by the spirit of that easy philosophy which distinguishes the race. Worn out by the struggle to break the force of the carelessness and destructiveness of his employé, he gradually reaches the conclusion that it is impossible. His eye at last is not affronted by the general confusion and lack of neatness in his immediate surroundings ; he is now disposed to suffer things to remain as they are, as the burden of altering them, by putting them in a condition of order, will necessitate afterwards a protracted contest that will entail a degree of annoyance and vigilance that seem wholly out of proportion to the result to be attained. When he has been reduced to this state of mind, he and his laborers are in such sympathy that their relations are of the friendliest character.

There is one quality of the negro laborer which is now regarded with increasing favor by his employer, and that is his natural and unconscious conservatism. Owing to this trait, as long as he is left to direct his own conduct there is little danger of labor being thrown into disorder in the communities of which the members of his race form the larger proportion of inhabitants.[1] Strikes are

[1] The only danger lies in the possibility of his becoming the ignorant tool of white-labor organizations.

unknown among them, because they are happy and contented if they can secure the bare necessaries of life, and also because they have no disposition to organize and co-operate of their own motion, even to attain an object that will redound to the advantage of all. Their inclination is not to rebel for the purpose of extorting higher wages for their services, but rather to earn those wages with as little physical exertion as possible. In some measure this conservative spirit is due to their long subordination to the whites, which has fostered a subservient temper in them, but to whatever ascribable it is likely to strengthen their position in the community, and, therefore, have a beneficial influence on their material condition. In consequence of this spirit they have a strong hold upon the good-will of the large planter, who, although he may express an unfavorable opinion of them in many of the relations of life, yet readily acknowledges their value to him as laborers. As such, they appeal to his selfishness, and however open to censure and criticism in many respects, their importance in this character gives them a claim upon his consideration which is not very much lessened by their deficiencies as men and citizens. For this reason such an employer, although he will animadvert severely on the general weaknesses of the race, and express his fear as to the harm that such an enormous mass of alien people, who are distinguished for none of those qualities that sustain civilization, except mere physical strength, will do to the section of country in which they are found, will yet earnestly deprecate any movement that looks to their emigration in great numbers. The economic tie between the negro laborer and the large planter is the only one that unites the two ; but this makes them dependent upon each other to an important extent, in the present age at least, in spite of those influences of mere race that lead them to separate socially and politically ; and this is an assurance that the negro is treated with substantial justice.   It is only as a workingman that he adds to the wealth and augments the general prosperity of the community.   If he were to lose his efficiency as such, or were to show any desire to disorganize labor, then his only element of usefulness to the land-owners and to society would be destroyed.   The bond that now attaches him to them would be broken ; he would become wholly isolated and defenseless, and would have no recognized position ; in consequence of which his presence would be regarded as an unmitigated evil.   The final result could only be disastrous to himself, for as soon as his rapid decline as a laborer sets in his decadence as a man begins.   That decline is already observable, but it is to the interest of the large land-owners at least that he shall not become entirely worthless in this character, this interest being abetted by the necessity that he is under to work ; and this necessity will only be more inexorable as the horde of his race increases.   In this interest of the principal land-owners, as well as in this compulsion, lies the salvation of the negro, for several generations, undoubtedly, not only as a workingman, but as an individual and a citizen.   His standing in the community, while he remains in it, will be secure as long as he is docile, industrious, and conservative ; his decay will be in proportion to his gradual loss of these qualities.

XIII.

MATERIAL CONDITION OF THE LABORER.

WHAT is the material condition of the laborer? An answer to this question involves an examination of the practical character of the negro, as well as of the opportunities that he has of securing the ordinary comforts of life. A brief study of the masses of the race reveals that they have many qualities that stand directly in the way of their material improvement even in the narrowest sense of the term; it may even be said that they have many qualities that render such improvement apparently impossible. Whether these qualities are wholly indigenous, or whether they are partially due to the institution of slavery that both provided for the slave and removed all incentive to prudence by taking away its reward, is open to discussion. The probability is that slavery merely fostered certain qualities that were already highly developed in the negro; for when we come to inquire into his condition wherever he has always been free, there we find him remarkable, substantially, for the same traits, traits that have either directly prevented him from rising above barbarism, or which at least have not assisted him to do so. The most unfortunate of these traits are carelessness, improvidence, and destructiveness. To a certain extent his transportation to America (although he was brought hither only as a slave) elevated him at once, economically speaking, because it raised his standard of physical comfort. The material aspirations of the American negro of to-day, as differentiated from his material condition, are certainly higher than those of his African kinsmen, since he has passed his whole life in close contact with white people, and has adopted their ideas very largely. His material condition, however, is not strikingly superior to that of the African blacks. Like the latter he lives contentedly amid surroundings that would be revolting to sensibilities of the least refinement. Even where an individual is found who chafes against such environment, it is observed that he is kept in the position which he dislikes by those ungovernable qualities to which I have already referred. The exception is when the negro is not distinguished for these qualities, and it is doubtful as to which of the three obstructs his improvement most. By carelessness I mean not merely heedlessness and lack of attention, but also that spirit of indifference which accepts a mean lot with an acquiescence that is not disturbed by any desire to rise to a higher condition, or that is not led to repine against the narrowness of destiny. Many negroes have a fluctuating ambition to advance their fortunes, but this ambition rarely causes them to repress the characteristics that thwart their wishes, and it still more rarely makes them dissatisfied with their present situation. The individuals of the race take life with an unconscious and spontaneous philosophy, happy if they can get food enough to supply the wants of the body, and contented as long as they have the roof of a cabin to protect them from the weather, wood with which to kindle a fire on the hearth, and clothes with which to conceal their nakedness. In the midst of the lowest circumstances they live in a state of complacency that is little shaken either by the ordinary cares peculiar to human life, or by those which, it would be supposed, would be incidental to their humble condition. As long as they can earn sufficient to enable them to obtain the few articles that they need, they do not think that they have any ground for complaint. Fortunately for them, their credit is generally restricted to the amount of their wages, and when the limit of that credit is reached, they are compelled to shift as they can, which they do without any apparent loss of cheerfulness.

A much more lamentable quality is their improvidence, a quality which has its origin in that carelessness of nature to which allusion has been made. This quality was very much fostered by slavery, and it has also been nourished by the influences that slavery transmitted to this age ; but it is probably indigenous, being an out-growth of that childishness which crops out in every phase of the general character of the negro. It is one of the most conspicuous traits of his mind, that it dwells on the present alone ; he does not learn by experience from the past to make provision for the future, and the conse-quence is, that in his desire to accomplish his immediate purpose he overlooks the injury that he may be doing himself in the light of a time that has not yet arrived. In many respects he resembles the common sailor, being ready to throw away in brief self-indulgence the fruits of his patient toil and long endurance of harsh conditions, and when these fruits are spent he is not racked by the pangs of regret. It may be asserted, without overstate-ment, that his inclination to gratify his tastes in those ways that money allows is only circumscribed by the limitation put upon his freedom of purchase by the per-son who seeks to make the most of his improvidence in selling him the various articles he wishes to buy. The number that he will take on account is only restricted by the prudence of his creditor. If he were permitted, he would thus bind himself on a single occasion to an amount that would not only absorb his annual wages, but plunge him so deeply in debt that it would be impossible for him to extricate himself afterwards ; and he would do this, not from any lurking hope that he can elude his creditor when pressed to pay, but in a spirit of general extravagance. There is no article that he will not purchase, however absurd in itself or however useless to him. Let it but strike his fancy, and the more gaudy and showy it is, the more forcibly does it appeal to his imagination. If he has no cash to give in return for it, he will be anxious to have it set down to his credit, and will earnestly deprecate a refusal to do so on the part of its owner. Even if the income of the negro increases for any reason, his expenses not only keep step with the sum that he is paid, but the improvement in his fortunes is apt to make him, if possible, still more improvident ; and it is not improbable that he will be more pinched as a man of fair pecuniary resources than he was as a common laborer working for slender wages.

The spirit of wastefulness in his general affairs takes in the course of his daily life the form of destructiveness. This characteristic of his nature is a great drawback to the use of improved machinery in the ordinary operations of the farm or plantation. He is disposed to run the reaper against a stump if it is situated conveniently, or to drive the mower against a stone ; he is not inapt to allow a stick to crash through the drum of the steam thresher ; and if he has been trained to act as the engineer in charge of the boiler, there is much danger of his suffering the pressure to rise so high as to result in a fatal explosion. It is found to be quite impossible to keep glass in the windows of any cabin which he inhabits. It would furnish a glazier almost uninterrupted occupation to renew the panes of the windows of many such cabins whenever they were broken. Not long after these panes are first put in, each window-frame will be observed to present a very motley aspect, patches of quilting, torn linen, pieces of old clothing, and faded newspapers being discovered in the spaces where glass formerly was. The same destructive instinct is exhibited in the facility with which the negroes will burn up the dry rails of all the fences in their vicinity ; they will often transport very valuable plank from a long distance to convert it into fuel, or they will tear from their cabins, for the same purpose, all the boards that can be thus used without exposing themselves to the severity of the weather.

With these unhappy qualities, which are found in all the individuals of the race, with few exceptions, it would be impossible for the laborers to improve their condition, even if the opportunities of earning money were numerous. The means of securing a livelihood at least is within the reach of all ; and if they could only acquire habits of prudence and economy, there is no reason why they should not be in the possession of every substantial comfort, but unfortunately these virtues are rarely observed in them, however industrious. The rates of wages range from eighty to a hundred dollars a year with rations, or eight to ten dollars a month, or forty to fifty cents a day. Cradlemen, ditchers, assorters of tobacco are paid higher for the same length of time, while women, girls, and boys receive from twenty-five to forty cents, whether they work in the fields or barns.

restlessness of the laborers by creating a definite reason why they should wish to leave the neighborhood.

The total advantages, in various forms, that the ordinary laborer in steady employment enjoys, are considerable, independently of his wages. In the first place, he is supplied without charge with rations in a sufficient quantity to satisfy the wants of his family and himself. As a rule, he chooses the plainest fare, perhaps because the work he does, calls for food of the strongest and most nourishing sort ; he, therefore, prefers bacon and the meal of the Indian corn to beef and flour ; and this is fortunate for himself, as the price of the former is much less, in proportion to quantity, than that of the latter. The regular allowance to an ordinary hand is 12 pounds of bacon and 5 pecks of meal by the month, or 144 pounds of bacon and 60 pecks of meal by the year, which, if he had to purchase them, would cost him twenty-three dollars in the course of twelve months. In addition to his rations, which are furnished to him as an important part of what he earns in compensation for his services, he is granted certain valuable privileges. Thus, he is always permitted to fatten two hogs at least, which generally reach a great size, as they are fed on the refuse of his cabin, and on the nutritious weeds that he cuts down along the banks of the streams. An acre of land, in the immediate vicinity of his dwelling, is assigned to him as a garden ; and here, by the labor of a few hours, he can produce many kinds of vegetables in profusion, such as beets, peas, potatoes, melons, cabbage, and tomatoes, which he eats as they ripen, or stores away for winter consumption according to variety. Furthermore, he is frequently allowed to cultivate little patches of corn, either in plats of ground near his house, or on parts of the plantation or farm to which he is attached that are not in tillage. The wages that he is paid in money is increased by the amount which he receives for the eggs and the fowls that he sells, a purchaser being found in the country merchant or the planter or farmer himself ; or these articles of food can be used to supply his own table.

These various comforts are within the reach of every industrious negro if he manages his general affairs with economy ; if he fails to secure them, it is because he dislikes to work steadily for any one employer, or is indifferent to his own prosperity. By a proper disposal of his narrow income, he can even obtain what would be considered by laborers of other countries to be the greatest luxuries. All the articles that he desires, whether to gratify his actual wants or his idle tastes, can be purchased at the nearest store, for the stock of goods on hand there was bought with a view to his needs and fancies alone. The variety of this stock is quite bewildering, representing, as it does to a limited extent in each direction, the goods to be found in a general combination of city shops. The country store, in fact, is an establishment in which few articles of merchandise are wanting ; there are groceries and sweet meats, liquors and medicines, trinkets, clothing and calicoes, pictures and toys, leather and tin in every form, wooden-ware, earthen-ware and hardware. While the prices at which these different kinds of goods are retailed realize a handsome percentage on the sums paid for them at wholesale, still the amounts for which they are sold do not draw too largely upon the resources of the negroes, otherwise the custom of the merchant would soon fall off so much as to lead to his bankruptcy. An excellent suit of clothing can be bought for six dollars, and the negro only needs two suits a year ; a pair of shoes can be purchased for two dollars, and a pair of stout boots for three.   A hat entails an expense of fifty cents, and its owner will consider it fit to be worn for an indefinite time.   Calico sells for seven cents a yard, and other articles in feminine use can be secured at proportionate figures ; coffee is rated at thirteen cents a pound, sugar at eight cents, flour at four.   All other groceries can be obtained according to the same scale of prices.   Articles of furniture and household utensils are sold quite cheaply, and are within the limits of the laborer's purse, provided that he has not exhausted its contents already in an improper way.   An examination of his monthly account discloses that the greater part of his wages has been spent in small luxuries with which he could dispense, or in mere trifles.   The most important items of this kind, are whiskey and ginger cakes.   It is not going too far to say that the majority of laborers waste in these two forms of physical indulgence money enough in the course of ten years to have purchased for each one the historic imaginary apportionment of forty acres and a mule.   The sums expended in whiskey are especially large, and yet it is rare to find among the negroes a confirmed drunkard, perhaps because their pecuniary resources are so narrow that they cannot gratify the appetite for liquor as uninterruptedly as they would like, and also because they are compelled by their situation to work for a livelihood ; nevertheless, the amount that they spend in dram-drinking is out of proportion to their means as well as their necessary expenses.   The adoption of a general prohibitory law would, no doubt, lessen if it would not put an end to this kind of extravagance, but

the negroes would be little aided pecuniarily by such a
law, as their money would be squandered in some other
way.

Independently of the country store, the laborer rarely
becomes indebted to any one except his employer; there
is generally a running account between the two, but this
account does not extend beyond the ordinary necessaries
of life. Occasionally the laborer purchases flour or
small supplies of beef and mutton from the planter, but
the latter does not, on the whole, find it either profitable
or convenient, although the body of men under contract
to him may be very large, to furnish them systematically
with those simple luxuries, or those articles that appeal
to their fancy only, which they are so ready to buy. It
is rare that an estate is inhabited by a sufficient number
of blacks to justify the erection of a store by its owner,
for the purpose of enjoying the benefit of their trade
alone.

The negro, however, runs little risk of being improperly treated as a customer by the country merchants, for
they all thrive upon his earnings; indeed there is much
competition among them to obtain his patronage, special
advantages being offered as an inducement to secure his
good-will. So numerous are the stores in a populous
country side, that he has always a choice of trading at
any one of two or three, and he selects the one that
allows him the easiest terms. He would prefer to make
his purchases at a store to dealing with his employer
directly, not only because such an establishment presents
a tempting variety of goods, but also because it serves
very largely as a club, where many of his fellows gather
after nightfall, both to buy what they need, and to exchange the freshest items of gossip and to tell the latest

joke. They rarely, under these or any other circumstances, enter into bargains of sale with individuals of
their own race, for they distrust one another's word too
much to be contented with a promise as the only basis
of exchange. It is only infrequently that they sell any
thing to each other for cash even, as they have little
ready money ; and then, too, the articles that they
would thus buy can be easily gotten on credit at the
neighboring store.

If we visit the homes of the laborers on all the plantations in the same section, we find that their material condition is similar everywhere, as a rule, although occasionally a marked difference is observed both in the character
and the surroundings of their cabins. On many of the
large plantations, that remain very much as they were in
the age of slavery, these cabins are arranged in the form
of a street, a considerable number of such structures
being erected either in the immediate vicinity of each
other, with the space of but a few feet between them, or
they stand apart at intervals of forty or fifty yards.
These are the quarters of slavery times, which still exist
as a lingering reminder of a régime that has passed away.
Many of the cabins of these quarters were built origi-
nally of the best material, and in the most thorough
manner, and will last in excellent condition for many
decades still. Some were even built of brick, and as
such will endure practically for an indefinite time, but the
use of brick for this purpose was quite rare. Generally
they are of wood, either in the form of hewn logs or of
common plank. The cabins on many of the farms and
plantations are not all found in the vicinity of each
other, but are separated into distinct groups of two or
more, that have a long distance intervening between

them. A cabin is sometimes discovered in the midst of
the forest, with no other house within a mile of its site. As
a rule, however, the dwellings of the laborers are erected
where they will be situated conveniently to the barns and
stables.

Throughout the whole of the tobacco region of Virginia, the eye of the traveller lights upon the domiciles
of the negroes at every opening in the woods or turn of
the road ; and they range in character from the meanest
hovel to the plain but substantial cabin. A more dreary
and uncomfortable habitation than the former could
hardly be conceived by the imagination. Such a hut is
always constructed of pine logs from which the bark has
not been stripped, the open space between them being
filled in with the tenacious red clay of the country. The
chimneys are made of sticks, sustained and protected by
the same natural plastering ; the original earth constitutes
the flooring ; rough stones take the place of iron dogs on
the hearth. An iron pot, a frying-pan, a few plates of
the coarsest manufacture, a few knives with horn handles,
are the only utensils and ware ; while a bed, a table, and
a couple of chairs or stools, all more or less shattered,
are the only furniture. The plank ceiling, which has a
tendency to sway towards the middle, can be touched
with the fingers without difficulty. In one corner the
meal box is generally placed, while in the other the
family tub stands on its bench. A pair of rickety steps
leads up to a dark garret, in which a variety of articles
are stored away, such as ragged clothing, broken chairs,
tools, the corn that has been gathered from the field near
the house, and the winter vegetables. However poor
the household may be, there are three things which it
never lacks—namely, wood for the fire, fresh water, and

pure air.   The window and door are always open, and
the cracks between the logs in the mud plastering are
often large enough to admit the hand ; hickory, oak, and
pine grow close by, and from the spring in the neighboring ravine there wells up perennially water as cool as the
soil of the earth through which it flows.

Occasionally a cabin that is quite substantial in appearance is observed, being built of large hewn logs,
properly plastered, the chimneys of stone, the roofs
closely shingled, the flooring of smooth planks, the fire-
places open and commodious, the furniture excellent
and well preserved.   Around the walls are tacked
pictures from illustrated papers or books ; here and
there, too, a bunch of dried pepper or other seed plant
is hung, or a hare or opossum skin.   In the immediate
neighborhood of such a cabin there is usually a garden
full of every kind of vegetable ; also a few apple, peach,
and cherry trees.   Not infrequently, too, there are
flowers, the favorite being the flaring sun-flower, that is
supposed to keep off the floating germs of malaria that
rise from the marshy watercourses.   The clothes-line
displays the abundant wearing apparel of the household.
At a short distance off the pig-sty is erected, not always
far enough away, however, for the wind to intercept its
pungent odors.   Here the family hogs are fattened on
the succulent weeds of the country, such as wild parsley
and the buffalo cane, or the refuse of the table boiled in
a mess in the pot.   Chickens, ducks, and turkeys run
about in search of food, and here and there lounges a
cur or hound that springs up with loud and fierce barks
as the stranger approaches.

The families of the negroes, as a rule, live upon the
coarsest fare, served in the plainest way, and there is

little difference in the character of their daily meals ; bacon and corn bread constitute the staple of their food in the morning and evening alike, and the meat is eaten from the utensil in which it is cooked, quite frequently without the assistance of any thing less primitive than the fingers and a common knife. There is observed, however, among many, especially among those who have grown up since the close of the war, a marked desire to improve and vary the character of their fare ; much of their earnings in consequence is wasted in victuals and luxuries which they cannot afford. Instead of increasing their comforts directly by raising poultry, enlarging their gardens, and by general good management, they devote such money as they can acquire to the purchase of expensive groceries which they could do without, or which they should not buy, unless their wages were higher or these wages were augmented by other pecuniary resources. In some of the cabins every table convenience is found, such as plates, dishes, knives, and forks, and the meals are neatly and substantially served. This superior style of living is noticed most often on the largest plantations, where the laborers enjoy many valuable privileges that are out of the reach of individuals who are employed in less favorable situations. If the traveller should grow hungry when the nearest tavern is still many miles away and no planter's home is in sight, he can probably obtain in the most prosperous of their dwellings what he will consider a fair meal, if his palate is not very fastidious. As soon as he states his wish, a table is drawn forward and a cloth spread over it ; on this a plate, knife, and fork are placed, and he is bidden to take a seat, with an apology for the necessary delay in preparation. In a few minutes the negro housewife has sifted the meal from the brand and kneaded a large cake, which she deposits near the centre of the fire after raking away the embers, and then covers it up with the hot ashes and live coals. Freshly laid eggs are brought from the hen-house, and set to frying with several slips of bacon in the frying-pan ; a young chicken is cast into the pot, or broiled on the gridiron ; potatoes, tomatoes, corn, peas, as the guest may prefer, are cooked ; and when all are ready, meat, eggs, and vegetables are dished and set on the board ; a glass of buttermilk is placed on one side of the plate, and the ash-cake, smoking hot and washed clean, on the other ; and the traveller is bidden to eat, while one of the children fans the flies away with a green bough. The rural feast is crowned with fruit, if the old-fashioned peach trees, that are usually planted around each cabin, are in bearing, and the fruit has ripened ; or, if not, then a cup of store coffee, that has been carefully put away for Sunday or a holiday, is substituted for it. The character of the meal would harmonize somewhat with the time of the year : if it were winter, a hare or opossum might be served up instead of the chicken, or some part of the pig that has only been lately slaughtered, or even a piece of beef or mutton, which the householder has recently bought from his employer.

There are few laborers who have as many opportunities to surround themselves in their homes with every reasonable comfort as the negroes of the tobacco region of Virginia, and if they fail to do so, it is owing to their improvidence, wastefulness, and indifference. Employment is easily obtained, and at such wages as to place even the luxuries of life in their reach, if they will only husband their resources ; there is so much untilled soil that every large planter allows his hands to cultivate considerable surfaces for their private use; fowls of every variety can be raised ; the woods and fields are full of many kinds of game that can be trapped ; the forests supply an abundance of fuel; and .there are stores wherever two public roads cross. In addition to these advantages, the blacks have their schools and churches, and they are so numerous as a people that they never lack social amusements. If they grow weary of one locality they can find work and a home elsewhere ; if they tire of one form of occupation, they can adopt another without any delay ; they can labor for wages or on shares as they prefer ; they can rent land on their own account; or they can seek the railroads, or settle in the towns and become house servants.

The condition of the few among them who show prudence and judgment is certainly superior to the condition of the lowest class of whites who, in our principal cities, toil in the unwholesome atmosphere of factories and pine with disease and poverty in small and filthy tenements. Let any one go into those parts of these great cities where this class lives. Let him mark their sallow and haggard faces, their sunken eyes and unclean persons—let him breathe the stifling air and smell the foul odors, and then suddenly let him be dropped down into the midst of a cluster of cabins on a prosperous plantation. Good-humored faces there surround him on all sides, and he sees contented dispositions reflected in every feature. His eye takes in at a glance the different signs of comfort about the homesteads, shabby and humble though they may be,—the pig fattening in the sty, the little patch of corn or tobacco, the peach and apple trees, the kitchen-garden, the pile of seasoned fuel, the umbrageous oak that shades the well trodden yard, the rustic spring with its connecting path, the poultry running in various directions, the children rolling in the dirt, the wife and mother cooking or sewing ; all being enveloped in the healthy air of the country that is laden with the fresh odors of the fields and forests. Does he doubt for a moment which of the two has most reason to be satisfied, the indigent workman of the town or the laborer who tills the green fields ?

The material improvement of the laborer is obstructed, as I have already remarked, by the fact that he is contented whether he is environed by all these comforts or not. His condition may be the reverse of that which I have described, and in the great majority of instances it is. His cabin may be a decayed shanty with a dirt floor, and with a hole in one side for a window,—a hovel as primitive as the hut of a Dinka or a Zulu ; its surroundings may show no evidence of the least thrift ; it may be without a garden, or corn patch, or pig-pen ; and yet it would be impossible to find a man who regarded existence with more placid happiness or more boisterous cheerfulness than its tenant does. No desire to rise troubles his brain, and no envy of those who are rich gnaws at his heart. The past has vanished ; the future has no existence ; it is the present alone that knocks at the door of his mind, and he is fully satisfied as long as he has enough bread and meat to keep him from starvation, a dilapidated coat to his back, an occasional dram, and the companionship of his friends. His philosophy is profound, but it is the unconscious philosophy of a man who is in the lowest state of nature.

XIV.

RENTERS AND LAND-OWNERS.

THE negro has an inclination towards agriculture, even apart from any liking for it which his life as a laborer has created and fostered ; this may, to some extent, be an inherited taste that had its origin in the special training of the individuals of many preceding generations. It has always been observed in the blacks throughout Africa. It was also noticed in the American slaves long before they were emancipated. To be allowed to have a garden, or to plant a few acres in corn, was regarded by them as a valuable privilege, irrespective of the addition thus made to their comforts ; and the same view is held by them, now that they are free, and are paid in wages, or have a share in the crop that they produce. This inclination is detected not only in the ordinary field hand, but also in the mechanic, and the house servant, whose duties have removed them from the influences that might have been thought to be the cause of it in the common laborer.

Like the peasant of every country, who earns his bread by tilling the soil, the negro has a desire to possess land. If unable to purchase it, he is anxious to rent as much as any proprietor is willing to lease to him. Indeed, he is never more contented than when he has acquired temporary control over a few acres ; it can be even said that he is happier situated thus than when he owns land, for

ownership lays upon his shoulders the burden of pro-
viding against taxation, besides leaving him without the
advice and support of a stronger and more experienced
person. His great satisfaction as a tenant is due to
various reasons. In the first place, he lives in entire
freedom from the pressure of any form of immediate
supervision ; he is not required to make his appearance
in the field at a stated hour, or to perform any task that
may be set him at a moment's notice ; on the contrary,
he can go to his work long after the sun has risen, and
no one will have the power to discharge him for his indolence. He can labor for as short a time as he likes, and
leave the field whenever he chooses ; he may hoe one
day and lounge the next ; or he may plough during two or
three days of the seven then mount his horse and visit a
neighboring community, where he can spend the remainder of the week. He can take part in excursions, attend
court, hunt, fish, or call at the store, as his passing mood
suggests. This ability to govern his own conduct, without being answerable to another's authority, is highly
valued by him, and he makes the most of it in so many
ways that he pays little heed to the condition of his
business. In his love of pleasure or in his laziness he
delays as long as possible to prepare the land for the
reception of the seed, and when he does put it in order
it is generally after an imperfect fashion. He often allows
the grass to spring up more rapidly than he cuts it down
with the hoe, and every successive phase in the growth
of his tobacco illustrates the same procrastinating spirit.
He shows, in the manipulation of his crop, after it has
been stored away in the barn, not only want of proper
attention, but of ordinary care and skill ; and the result
is that the grade which he places upon the market is

very inferior. In every county where much tobacco is produced by his fellow-tenants there has been a conspicuous decline in the quality of the staple. Whether his crop, however, is mean or excellent, or whether it pays the expenses of cultivation or not, he is so much pleased with the independence of his life that he is contented if he has been able to pass through the year with a fair degree of credit at his store. He is always eager to renew his lease if the owner of the land is willing to allow him to do so, for he is not in the least discouraged by the result of his agricultural operations during the previous twelve months.

At one time the planters were disposed to rent much of their land to negroes on shares, the general terms being that, if the proprietor furnished teams, forage, and implements, and cabin and fuel for tenant and his family, he was to receive one half to three fourths of what was made, the proportion varying with the fertility of the soil, the character of the crops, and other similar conditions. On the other hand, if the tenant supplied the teams and implements, which he was rarely able to do on account of his poverty, the proprietor was paid from one fourth to one third of the products. If the former only leased as many acres as he could cultivate himself, without the need of assistance in any form, the land-owner was satisfied if he secured an amount that would cover the rental of the cabin. So far has the system of leasing to the negroes failed in consequence of their carelessness, indolence, and unreliability, that there has been a great decline in its popularity. A proprietor rents to them now only as a last resort. This is one of the many instances of how much their unhappy qualities stand in the way of their material improvement, and how unequal

they are to taking advantage of the most favorable opportunities. If they were distinguished for prudence, judgment, and energy ; if they would devote their whole time
and attention to the business in which they are engaged ;
if they had, when left to themselves, any capacity for ac-
quiring skill in that business, by the closest study of its
requirements they could place themselves in a few years
in an independent position by renting land and cultivating tobacco. Land indeed is so abundant that its owners
would be glad to add to their incomes by leasing many
acres, that would otherwise lie idle, to colored tenants
who could be relied upon to use the soil well and pay
rent with some degree of certainty ; but whoever leases
to a negro understands that it signifies the further im-
poverishment of the soil, and at the same time it is doubtful whether there will be obtained in return a sum equal
to its annual depreciation in quality. The proprietor is
hampered by the presence of a lessee whom he cannot
directly supervise and control, and whose lax habits are
calculated to exercise a bad influence over the laborers
who are in the proprietor's employment. These laborers
observe that the tenant has much time at his disposal, in
which he can do precisely what his inclinations lead him
to do ; they see him directing his own hands, for he has
to hire a couple or more, or they notice him riding lei-
surely about on his own horse. The enjoyment of so
much independence, as well as of so much importance, by
one of their own race, who, they are aware, is no better
off in the point of capital than they are, has the effect of
raising their envy and, in a certain measure, of demoralizing them.

The greatest injury which a planter can inflict upon
the interests of the community in which he lives, is to

rent the whole of his estate in small lots to colored tenants, especially if he abandons his home permanently to
dwell elsewhere, leaving his property entirely in their
hands. The quality of the soil begins at once to depre-
ciate from improper usage and careless cultivation ; the
buildings and fences soon fall out of order from natural
decay or the depredations of pilferers ; the teams decline to the poorest condition ; the crops produced are
of an inferior quality. But this is not all : such an
estate soon becomes the safe harbor of all the depraved
negroes in the vicinity ; the vicious habits of the women
and men alike increase owing to their removal from the
control of the proprietor ; thievish and superstitious
practices are more common and open, and brawls and
quarrels arise more often than elsewhere. The relations
of the inhabitants with the whites in the surrounding
country grow strained and hostile, and their bearing insolent. In short, within the narrow confines of one
plantation, we observe all the unfortunate effects which
the isolation of the negroes to themselves invariably has
upon their disposition and conduct in every locality.

Many of the negroes who have acquired land of their
own in fee simple appear to more advantage than those
who simply rent it from white proprietors. One explanation of this is, that the latter act is very frequently a
mere device of indolence, the chief object of the lessee
being to escape from that protracted drudgery and unbroken routine to which a common laborer on a plantation has to submit. He wishes to shape his own conduct untrammelled by that authority to which he would
be subjected as a mere employé ; in other words, he desires to be in a position in which he can work or idle
away his time just as he may prefer. As a renter he is

at liberty to follow the promptings of his moods as they rise, and hence it is a condition that his easy disposition holds in high appreciation. On the other hand, the fact that a negro is a land-owner is a proof, as a rule, that he is superior in certain qualities of his character to the great mass of his race. He may not be stricter in morals or brighter in mind, but he is likely to be sounder in judgment, and to have more power of self-control. To hoard sufficient money to buy even a few acres, however cheaply they can be purchased, is fair evidence that he is comparatively steady and economical in his habits, prudent and careful in his views, and, above all, not only animated by ambition to improve his fortunes, an ambition shared by many of his people in a fluctuating way, but also (and this is far more important, and it is rarely remarked among his fellows) that he has self-restraint enough to realize that ambition. A man who has such aspirations, associated with sufficient strength of purpose to carry them into effect, is apt to display, when he comes into possession of an estate of his own, the same practical qualities that enabled him to secure it,—qualities that may lead to successful management. The flower of the race is to be found among these small land-owners, men who alone in the vast swarm of negroes who darken the country like an ominous cloud, give us the least confidence in its capacity.

When we examine the best type of these colored proprietors, we find them, almost without exception, to be freedmen of simple tastes, who were trained to be industrious, regular, and vigilant by the discipline that prevailed on the plantations under the régime of slavery. In many instances they were foremen, and were thus accustomed not only to command and superintend, but to bear the weight of responsibility, a still more useful form of education. This experience was of inestimable service to them when emancipation threw them on their own resources. Having been habituated to the plain style of life that had been enforced among them before they were freed, they had no desire to throw their earnings away in luxuries which they could not afford to purchase with their narrow wages. By laying aside a few dollars each month, they soon accumulated enough to buy small areas of land on the ridges that extend back from the watercourses ; this land they were able to acquire at very low rates, as it was quite worthless for the production of any crop except tobacco, which, also, could only be cultivated there with the assistance of fertilizers. On soil that is apparently too thin to sustain much growth of any kind, a fine quality of this staple can be raised with the aid of artificial manure. It was due to this fact alone that the various purchases of these freedmen were not wholly without value. The ground along the rivers and smaller streams was held at such a high price an acre, that not one among them was able to buy it, however careful and industrious, and, in consequence, they were compelled to settle on the highlands. This is the character of the tracts that even the most thrifty own. These tracts range from five to a hundred acres, some of them being in a fair state of cultivation in spite of their inferior quality ; the proprietors, in consequence of the training they received as slaves, comparing quite favorably in their methods and management with the class of small white planters. The estates of the freedmen who are most alert, thoughtful, and diligent are occasionally found to be as well appointed in the way of barns, cribs, and stables as the estates of their white neighbors, their teams in as high order, their fences in as good repair, and their tobacco crops as flourishing. The houses in which they live are plainly but substantially built ; an effort at some adornment is often detected both within and without them, the aspect of the surroundings being generally indicative of a considerable degree of comfort and prosperity.

An interest in land has, in a measure, had a beneficial effect on the more intelligent of the negro proprietors. In the first place, they have been forced to take the future into account, which has tended to inculcate habits of prudence. They also know that idleness signifies that it is only a question of time for them to be sold out by the public auctioneer for delinquent taxes ; and this has been calculated to make them both industrious and assiduous, apart from the mere necessity of earning a livelihood for themselves and their families. The responsibility which the exclusive care of their property places on their shoulders has given them little time to plume themselves on their superiority to the rest of their people. That flighty vanity observed in their fellows, with few exceptions, when elevated into importance, has not been so noticeable in them, for their position is more or less a precarious one, as it is dependent upon their own diligence and judgment whether they can sustain themselves. And if they have these sober qualities they are not apt to fall into a foolish conceit.

The more successful the colored land-owner is, the keener his appreciation of the stake that he has in the condition of the community is apt to be. The most respectable of these proprietors are, in fact, the only men among the negroes who seem to realize what citizenship means. The masses of the race are as alien to the soil as if they had just arrived from some foreign shore, with all their peculiarities as a foreign people still distinct, and feeling no concern about the prosperity of their adopted country, on account of their ignorance of its needs. They pay no taxes of any importance; apparently to them the administration of the government does not touch them at all, because it does not sensibly affect their selfish interests. But with the owner of a large number of acres, the case is likely to be different; his understanding must be strangely obtuse if he does not see very clearly how intimately his own financial condition is associated with the general welfare of his community; and there can be little doubt that the most intelligent of these colored proprietors perceive this, and are, in consequence, more thoughtful as citizens than they would otherwise be. Those among them who are skilful and successful, as well as sober and conservative, are regarded with respect by the whites, and are treated in personal intercourse as entitled to it. There is no prejudice against such men on account of their good-fortune; on the contrary, there is an earnest desire among the most influential members of the ruling class that the same qualities shall be exhibited by others, leading to the same acquisition of land and to a similar success in its management, for not until the negro becomes a property holder, not until he has an interest in the soil, do the whites expect to see him an estimable citizen, as much concerned as they are in a just and economical administration of public affairs, both State and local. While it is recognized that it is comparatively rare that individuals of the race have the capacity or the character to accumulate such property, yet it is hoped that those who succeed in doing so will form in time a body of men who will not only exert much influence by the example they set, but will also have power to restrain those elements among their own people from which so much is to be feared.

Although a few colored land-owners are found who are as successful as the majority of the smaller planters among the whites, yet only too many fail in their annual operations, not so much from indifference to their own interests, which is infrequently remarked, as it is necessary that they shall work to retain the property that they have, but rather from ignorance of correct methods of tillage, and from a lack of means with which to purchase the required manures. A more striking example of meanness of fortune is rarely observed than that presented by many of this class of negroes who have invested their little savings in a few acres that lie on the backbone of a vast ridge, far removed from every stream and apparently from all trace of civilization. Here, in the midst of the stunted forest, or at the edge of fields that have been abandoned as too impoverished to produce any kind of crop, and almost too poor to nourish a growth of briars or broomstraw, these indigent householders have erected primitive shanties and stables of logs and sticks. Their rude carts are of their own manufacture, with the exception of the wheels ; their teams consist of brindled oxen from the pine barrens and spavined mules which they have bought for a few dollars from the planters or at public auction ; their plows are old and broken ; their harness partly leather and partly rope ; their forage, the shucks and tops of such corn as they have been able to raise. Their land, to produce even a scanty subsistence, must have the aid of fertilizers. As they are unable to buy the artificial manures, it is often difficult to understand how they and their families eke out an existence. Maize will not spring up with any vigor in such soil as they own, and even in the most favorable season will form only the smallest nubbins. Their only hope lies in tobacco, and they cultivate this without being discouraged by the most meagre returns. They, their wives, and children, tattered, unwholesome, and forlorn in appearance, will be seen tilling their little patches, the plants of which do not hide the surface of the ground from view. By the crops which they thus secure, with the addition of the few vegetables which they obtain from their gardens, and of the animals that they trap or shoot in the neighboring woods, they keep their families alive, but the struggle to do so is harsh and continuous, and barely successful. And yet, precarious as their means and wretched as their surroundings are, they would not change their situation. They prefer to live as they do, striving for a scanty support on their own land, where they are at liberty to act as they choose, to working on the most extensive and prosperous of the adjacent plantations, although they know that there they will be promptly paid fair wages, that they will have comfortable cabins, large gardens, an abundance of fuel and nutritious food, and the society of several hundred people of their own color. They share this feeling with all the individuals of their race in whom the agricultural instinct is developed to an unusual degree, and who, with few exceptions, would settle in the most inaccessible spots, on narrow and impoverished tracts of land, rather than enjoy the most liberal compensation for their toil, as well as valuable privileges as laborers in the employment of the planters and under the supervision of overseers. They are influenced in this preference by the independence of the life which they would lead on their own estates, and also by that irregularity of effort which it permits.

The negroes of the tobacco region of Virginia have, since their emancipation, been afforded the most favorable opportunities of improving their condition by purchasing land. Its cheapness has put it in the power of every laborer to secure a small homestead, that could be made sufficiently productive to enable him to support his family, and even to accumulate some capital. It is the planter who owns a few hundred acres rather than a thousand or more, who has found the culture of tobacco most profitable, because he can till his soil and manipulate his crop more economically, as his working force is principally furnished by the members of his own family, and he can give every detail of his business his personal supervision. Up to the present day the negro laborers have, perhaps, been in receipt of more money[1] than any other class of the community; and if they had saved even a portion of their earnings, it could have been invested to the greatest advantage in the land, which the revolution in the general economic system, produced by the civil war, threw upon the market. If there had been any demand for such land on their part, they could have readily bought it at the lowest prices. There were few owners of estates off the watercourses who would not have consented to sell many acres, in order to contract the size of properties that had always been too large, as well as to obtain cash; and yet such opportunities of improving their condition at the very time that these opportunities have been fairest, have not been utilized by the masses of the blacks, not because they have failed to observe them, but

[1] In the form of wages.

because they have not had the qualities to provide the purchase money that was necessary. When we consider the extravagance and carelessness of the race, it is easy to understand why its members continue poor in the midst of those excellent openings for establishing themselves in permanent comfort that exist even now. The monthly account of each one with his merchant discloses how far such sums as he has earned have been thoughtlessly expended, which, if they had only been carefully laid by, would in time have enabled him to buy many acres in the neighborhood of the cabin in which he lived. The golden period of the negro, with respect to his ability to secure valuable tracts, has been the last twenty years when the depression in real estate has been greatest, in consequence of the transmitted influences of the war. An advance in this interest has now begun,[1] and this advance has been most noticeable in land that fifteen years ago was regarded as worthless, on account of the thinness of the soil ; this being due to the fact that such soil has been found to be suitable for the production of the most profitable varieties of tobacco. An acre that formerly sold for two dollars, has, in some counties, risen in value to fifteen. Many estates can still be bought at the former rate, but for the most part they barely yield a subsistence. They are not adapted to the finer kinds of tobacco, for if they were, they would be held at the highest price ; they are not fertile enough for wheat and corn, no manure being used in producing these crops.

An increase in the number of small white planters will diminish the ability of the negro to buy estates, because such increase implies an advance in the price of

---

[1] The general advance is due to the demand for land among small white planters who have accumulated ready money.

land, upon which the prosperity of the white people must always rest. This will only render it more difficult than ever for the blacks to acquire it. If few were able to make purchases in the period of the greatest depression of prices, that is, in the course of the last two decades, the probability is that still fewer will be able to do so in the future, on account of the general rise in valuations that will attend an improvement in the condition of the whites. So far as can be observed, the race is not more economical after twenty years of freedom than it was after five, or even ten; and its habits are not likely to change with the progress of time. There is also another fact that points to the improbability of its members obtaining possession of much real property in the future, namely, the remarkable disparity at the present day between the number of land-owners among the freedmen, and the number of land-owners among the members of the generation that has reached maturity since the close of the war. The largest proportion of the inhabitants of every community of the race belong distinctively to the period of freedom; negroes who were ten years old when emancipated, and who, therefore, could not have been very much affected by the influences of slavery, have now arrived at middle age; children have sprung up to manhood who have no recollection whatever of that institution; indeed the majority of all the active men, who are either laborers, mechanics, or teachers, at the present time, can be said to have no knowledge of any other system except that which has prevailed during the course of the last twenty years. Their characters have been moulded, and their habits formed under the pressure of the new era alone. And yet the number of those, of whom this is true who are owners of small tracts even, is remarkably insignificant as compared with the number of proprietors who were trained in early life under the old régime.[1] In wide sections of country, where, in the aggregate, a considerable extent of soil is held by the blacks, there are few land-owners to be found who have not passed their fiftieth year, unless they have inherited their little farms or plantations from their fathers, who were once slaves. The members of the race who have hoarded enough to buy small estates, have been able to do so in most instances, because they have occupied positions of responsibility on the larger plantations, to which higher wages than usual are attached. Such positions have been open to men who have grown up since 1865, as well as to the freedmen, but even when the former have risen to these positions, they have not been distinguished, on the whole, for the same degree of prudence and economy as the latter.

The disproportion in the number of land-owners of the older and younger generations respectively is due to various causes. It is due, in the first place, to the fact that emancipation itself has exercised a powerful stimulating influence over the general conduct of the former slave. His mere recollection of his condition before he was set at liberty must have inspired him with a strong desire to improve his fortunes even beyond those advantages which freedom in itself alone conferred. On the other hand, the individual of the new era has no remembrance of slavery as an institution. As he has been free from childhood, no other condition is known to him. There has been no great revolution in his life,

---

[1] The number of younger proprietors is very insignificant, even when regarded separately.

for he cannot recall a time when he was aware that he was the absolute chattel of another man. From the hour he came of age he has been working under contract for various employers, and he is content to continue to do so.

A still more obvious explanation of the success of the freedman is that fact to which I have already referred at various times—namely, that he was subjected at the most plastic and responsive period of his existence to the strict discipline of slavery, which cultivated in him industrious habits, regularity of life, and simple tastes ; above all, it repressed in him that fickle spirit which is so marked in his race, when its individuals are allowed the greatest latitude of action. It is the restlessness of the later generations that stand so much in the way of their improvement, for it increases their natural tendency to extravagance and improvidence, besides leading to an augmentation of their necessary expenses. To lay aside any part of their wages after paying all that they are forced to spend, demands of them the most careful watch over their conduct, the most vigilant repression of their appetites, the highest prudence and economy in the management of their affairs ; and this circumspection and discretion must be exercised daily and hourly. To accumulate even a fair amount, situated as they are, and with their narrow resources, might well tax men of the most parsimonious habits and the greatest practical sagacity. How much more difficult for themselves, who have small knowledge of any form of self-restraint, and little appreciation of the possible consequences of their acts ! Unhappy characteristics are far more logical in their operation than those that are happy. As the most unfortunate qualities of the race are found more fully developed in individuals of the new generation than in their fathers, because these individuals have never been brought under careful discipline, their worst traits having thus had full room for growth, the result has been that they own little property of any kind, although they live in a country and at a period when land is still selling at rates at which it can be easily purchased by them if they show any self-denial.   Prolonged effort and sober habits are absolutely essential to their success ; they are largely lacking in these traits now, and there is little to foster these traits in the future.   In the meanwhile, any rise in the prosperity of the community only obstructs still further the improvement of their condition by means of the cheapness of the soil, since any increase in that prosperity must be based, as I have stated, upon an advance in real estate.

XV.

MECHANICS.

BEFORE slavery was abolished, every plantation that extended over a large area, and the agricultural operations of which were conducted on an important scale, was supplied with mechanics from the ranks of the negroes attached to it. Each blacksmith, carpenter, wheelwright, and mason belonged, as a rule, to the planter for whom they were engaged in working. It was the custom to select those young men, who, from their intelligence, appeared to be most likely to become skilful in such trades, and to apprentice them to the various handicraftsmen who were employed in the plantation workshops, by whom they were trained, and under whose supervision they continued until death or old age removed the instructors, whose place they then took, teaching in their turn young men of promise. The field of these mechanics, however, was not one in which they could acquire the highest dexterity and ingenuity in their respective pursuits, admitting that they were careful and exact enough in character to do so under favorable circumstances. Their attention was confined entirely to the common requirements of the plantation : the duty of the smith, for instance, being to shoe the mules and horses, to make and mend tires, and to rivet bolts ; the mason having to lay and cement the foundations of barns and stables, and to raise stone walls ; the carpenters to build cabins and sheds, shingle roofs, and construct hogsheads.   They rarely passed to more difficult forms of work in their special lines, as they had not the necessary experience.   When complicated machinery got out of order, or parts of manufactured farm implements were broken or destroyed, and had to be replaced, or when houses were to be erected after ambitious architectural designs, it was generally necessary to secure the services of white men who followed their trades in the neighboring towns.   And yet within the limits of their capacity, no slaves played a more useful part in the economy of the plantation than the black mechanics ; they were really indispensable, as a serious emergency might arise at any moment when their skill and knowledge would have to be applied with the greatest promptness to prevent delay in the progress of the agricultural operations.   The larger estates were so isolated locally, and their respective communities were so distinct, that it would have been inconvenient for the planters to have hired their mechanics to each other by the job, even if each planter had not always needed those he owned. Under the old system, however, many negroes were trained in handicraft with a view to hiring them out permanently, as the compensation for their services returned a very fair percentage on their value as slaves.   These men were obtained under the terms of regular contracts, being provided for, however, as if they belonged to the persons who engaged them.   Many of them were taken to the cities, where they were often employed in doing much more important work than would have been assigned to them on a plantation.   In general, however, they were found in the country villages and towns, or on the smaller estates whose proprietors had comparatively

their respective lines in a wide section of country, and, therefore, must have a higher skill and a more thorough knowledge than is possessed by the men who, as slaves, were only taught to meet the most ordinary plantation requirements.

Colored masons are not very numerous outside of the towns and cities, since their trade is one that does not offer very much employment in rural communities ; such stonework as has to be done in the erection of houses being performed by the men who put the frames together.

While the number of mechanics who were instructed as slaves has been curtailed, not only by the withdrawal to other pursuits, of many who were thus educated, but by the operation of natural causes during the course of twenty years, nevertheless the places which they vacated have not been filled to any great extent by members of the generation that has been accustomed only to the influences of freedom. Indeed, one of the most discouraging features of the character of the negroes who have grown up since the war is their extreme aversion to the mechanical trades. Very few of the younger men become carpenters, blacksmiths, or masons of their own accord, those who adopt these trades being, as a rule, the sons of fathers who were brought up as mechanics by slave-holders. These sons were compelled in their early youth, by the paternal authority, to assist at the tasks of the workshop or the smithy, and have remained in the same line by the force of habit. Many who might have been carefully instructed, relinquished the opportunity opened to them as soon as they were old enough to support themselves, at which time they emigrated to a distance, and entered employments that were congenial to their tastes. The explanation of this antipathy on their part to mechanical pursuits is easily found ; such pursuits constrain them to conform more closely than they like to a steady routine of work which is most arduous and trying, on the whole. The duties of a hand on a plantation are neither easy nor light, it is true, but these duties are constantly changing with the progress of the seasons ; they may necessitate the greatest toil during one month, and be attended with comparative relaxation of effort during another. Above all, the laborer is not tied down to one spot ; if he grows weary of one locality, he can find occupation elsewhere. But this is not the position of the young mechanic ; his success is largely dependent upon his remaining in one place ; he secures patronage by winning a reputation for skill and assiduity in his trade, and it is not in his power to earn such a reputation as long as he yields to his inclination to wander. When he moves from one neighborhood, he is not at all assured that he will obtain employment in his line in another, as the only stand there may have been taken, and, at best, he will be unknown and friendless.

Even when a young negro has been trained by his father, who was formerly a slave, he finds it difficult to compete with white men, because his mechanical education has been of the rudest character, and limited to the simplest branches of his trade. It is in smithcraft alone that he would have a wide and favorable field, since this occupation is generally left to the individuals of his race, but it is the very one from which the average young negro shrinks with the greatest aversion, as it is the most exacting and confining of all the mechanical pursuits. Wielding the heavy hammer hour after hour would put his strength to a test as searching as that which tries the endurance of a convict who is compelled

to crack stones on the highway. In the mere arduous-
ness of the labor which it requires, the life of a smith
who is attentive enough to his business to earn a living
by it, is more severe than that of a slave ; and, in addition
to this, his hours of work are much more protracted than
they are in the instance of negroes who follow other
employments. His smithy is most frequently located
near a store, the principal customers of which are only
able to visit it in the late afternoon, or after night has
fallen. His patronage is largely obtained from these
customers, and he has to be careful to accommodate
himself to the hours that are most convenient for them
to utilize his skill ; he is thus often detained in his shop
long after the laborers, who have been engaged in the
fields, have dropped their hoes or abandoned their plows
and returned to their cabins.

The places of a few of the mechanics who were trained
under the old régime, have been taken by young
negroes who were educated in industrial schools, and
who afterwards decided to settle in the secluded rural
districts. These young men perform their work with a
fair measure of skill, and are not deficient in assiduity ;
when attentive to their business, and animated by a
desire to advance in it, they find no difficulty in securing
an extensive and valuable patronage. Quite frequently,
however, they show that restlessness of spirit, that long-
ing for a change which is observed in the individuals of
their own age and race at large, and this has the effect of
diminishing their usefulness and injuring their prosperity.
Having been taught in a school, and having, to a certain
extent, been brought into contact with the world, they
are not as contented in the comparative retirement of the
country as they would be if they had been instructed in

their trades by the plantation mechanics, but at the same
time they are better fitted to meet all the mechanical
needs of the localities in which they may be. Their
usual ambition is to live in the most populous communities, as, for instance, in towns and villages, not so much
because they have a wider field there, which they really
have not, owing to the competition of white men, but
rather because the society of such communities is more
agreeable to their tastes.

Negroes who have been educated in industrial schools
are, however, very rare. In consequence of this, as well
as of the fact that the individuals of the race are not inclined to adopt mechanical pursuits, these pursuits, as
the mechanics among the freedmen die, are in the rural
districts gradually falling into the hands of the whites.
This is more especially the case now with the trades of
the carpenter, wheelwright, and mason. The blacks who
are employed in these trades are, as a rule, mere assist-
ants of white men, and do only the humblest parts of the
labor required, such as raising the logs and stones into
position, or sawing and planing the plank. Their relation to their superiors is such, that they are not likely to
learn on their own account how to take absolute charge
of any important work, and conduct it to a successful
conclusion. They are not apprentices in the true sense
of the word, being simply selected for their physical
strength, without regard to their having capacity enough
to assume control of any special task without advice, and
on their own responsibility. Throughout the tobacco
region the buildings most commonly observed are barns,
which demand no special architectural skill in their con-
struction. Of all the innumerable buildings of this kind,
scattered throughout a wide section of country, that have

236 THE PLANTATION NEGRO AS A FREEMAN.

been put up in the last ten years, perhaps twenty in
every five hundred have been raised by colored
men who have had exclusive management. Not one
of the various dwelling-houses, inhabited by the
white planters of many counties, was designed by a
black mechanic, and erected under his supervision.
Here, as elsewhere, the weakness of the negro when
thrown upon his own resources is notable, however
far his skill in handiwork may have been developed ; he
may have sufficient knowledge of his business to make
an excellent assistant, but he cannot, as a rule, be relied
upon in exacting circumstances to direct without close
superintendence. Even in the mechanical trades he
shows that lack of the power of intellectual combination,
that want of the capacity for originating, which is detected in the members of his race in every situation in
which they are placed. The only trait of those who
have been specially trained, which is at all encouraging
in its bearing on their capacity to attain to the highest
skill, is that they frequently show pride in their work, a
pride which, it must be admitted, is not always associated
with unusual excellence, but this pride might be made
the basis of the acquirement of greater dexterity. In the
mechanical pursuits, that peculiar heedlessness which
distinguishes the negro, that inexactness which is so
patent in all that proceeds from his hands as well as
from his mind, has been found to be the principal drawback to his improvement ; and this obstacle has been
more conspicuous here, as the opposites of these qualities
are so essential. These qualities, however, are more apt
to be repressed by him now than they were formerly,
because, in the present age, he has to rely so largely on
his own merits. He must be both skilful and attentive

to obtain work, for if he is ignorant and negligent, he is likely to suffer so much in consequence that it will only be a question of time for him to be forced to abandon his trade. So far, however, the negro has shown no disposition to provide against future misfortunes to himself by removing, through an effort of will and closer attention to the details of his business, those deficiencies that do so much to jeopardize his welfare. He resigns himself as cheerfully to the inevitable results of his own injudicious acts or general weaknesses of character as if he were unable to prevent them ; and he is as likely to display this trait in a mechanical pursuit as in any other that he may follow. It would be difficult for him, therefore, to hold his own in such a pursuit in the point of skill, if he were compelled to compete with resolute and careful white men. This is not only true of him in the trades, but also in every position of life. The negro has a tendency now to become either a laborer or a house servant, because in these capacities he is removed from all serious rivalry on account of certain qualities of character that distinguish him, such as docility, amiability, and perfect contentment in the humblest situations. If he were dissatisfied and ungovernable, he would begin at once to lose ground even in those pursuits which he now virtually monopolizes, for this would bring him into competition with the whites. As a mechanic his position is much more precarious, because he is not naturally adapted to it by the turn of his mind and nature. There is only one means of multiplying the number of negro mechanics, as well as of preparing them in the way of expertness and trustworthiness for the more stringent conditions that now confront them, and that is the technical school. Undoubtedly many individuals of the race will continue to be educated by local apprenticeships, but without the assistance of such schools fewer will be trained every year, until finally those who are trained will bear the most insignificant proportion to those who are employed merely as laborers. An increase in the prosperity of the country would have the same effect in contracting the circle of colored mechanics as it would have in diminishing the class of colored land-owners ; there would be a demand for greater aptitude, a demand that would augment the number of white mechanics, who could, without any difficulty, compete successfully with unskilled blacks in the same business. The technical school would place the latter in a much better position to meet this competition, and would thus give their race a fair proportion of those who follow these trades. In such an institution the individual negro could be instructed as far as his natural capacity might allow him to be. If he had any native bent towards such pursuits, it could there be strenuously encouraged. Not only would its course be better adapted to prepare him for the work that he has to do than a mere apprenticeship under a local carpenter or mason who was trained as a slave, or as the son of a former slave, but the discipline prevailing in such an institution would be apt to counteract those weaknesses of his nature which would prevent him from being proficient if he was accustomed only to the lax methods of a rural workshop. Habits of industry would be fostered in him by an unbroken routine of industrial duties. The idea would be inculcated that his career in life was to be confined to mechanical tasks, and he would be so carefully and closely drilled that this idea would become fixed in his own mind. There would be nothing to divert his attention during the time of his instruction. He would neither have an opportunity of shirking his duties nor throwing them up altogether by a sudden withdrawal. And if the school were to consummate the training thus given by securing the graduate a stand in some prosperous locality, the good that it would accomplish would be of lasting advantage.

It would not be well to overstock the various trades by thus educating too many negroes to follow them ; but a long time would be required for the supply to reach the limit of the demand. The establishment of technical schools for the blacks by the act of the State would mean the establishment of similar schools for the whites, but many years must elapse before the field in which their respective graduates would work would become so contracted as to bring them into direct conflict. In a contest between white and black mechanics of equal skill, the latter might compete successfully with the former, in consequence of the fact that they would be contented with a meaner style of life, which would enable them to charge at the lowest rates ; but if they could not hold their own in such a contest they would have to submit to that great economic law that drives the weakest to the wall, which can neither be resisted nor questioned. This is a law that touches individual, class, and race alike ; a law that has no mercy or sentiment, either in nature or society, and yet producing in its operation all that is most valuable and permanent in civilization.

The best field for the negro mechanic in the future will be, as it has been in the past, in that great section of country where the plantation system still prevails. It has been urged in favor of the establishment of technical schools for the black population, that they would tend to shift that population more evenly throughout the Union,

as the graduates of such schools would seek those localities where there was room for their services, irrespective
of State lines. It is doubtful whether colored mechanics
could, in considerable numbers, attain to a secure position outside of the South. Elsewhere they would be
brought into conflict with white workingmen, who are slow
to admit them to their own circle, even when they have
skill and assiduity to recommend them. Wherever white
people largely predominate the negroes can only sustain
themselves by becoming house servants or by performing
the lowest kinds of labor. In every other occupation
they have many obstacles to surmount in such communities, which they are not adapted by their natural capacity
or past history or present position as a race to overcome.
If they are to rise as handicraftsmen to respectability in
the general order of society, it must be in that section
of the republic where the blacks are so numerous that the
greater portion of all manual tasks is left to them by the
mere force of necessity, and where these mechanics
would be able to establish themselves without being
confronted at once by any rivalry of fatal importance.
Here they would always have a large share of the patronage of certain trades, and would, for some reasons, have
as fair a chance as white men of maintaining themselves
in all.

XVI.

FUTURE OF THE NEGRO.

I.

In the course of my previous discussion of the different branches of my general subject, I have stated briefly and incidentally what I anticipated the future of the plantation negro in Virginia would be, whether considered from a moral, social, or political point of view. In the first section of my final chapter I shall endeavor to arrange these disconnected opinions in a systematic form with due regard to their natural relation, as far as they bear any relation to each other at all. To describe the condition of the blacks, even as it is found to be to-day, is a task attended with many difficulties and perplexities ; but when we come to speculate upon their destiny as a people we soon perceive that we have entered a wide field of conjecture. If we restrict the scope of our vision somewhat, the ground does not seem so uncertain in the light of definite tendencies of the negro at this time that are likely to be followed hereafter by their logical consequences. After all, the principal element of doubt in our contemplation of his future is not so much whether these tendencies will be modified by any alteration in his fundamental character, as whether they will be held in check by circumstances, or whether they will override circumstances, however strong the opposition offered.

The most conspicuous, and in its bearing on their future, the most significant influence at work among the plantation negroes of Virginia is that which is withdrawing the two races further and further from each other ; and their disposition to move apart will be stronger still when the freedmen now living have vanished from the stage. Indeed, their social separation will be so wide in the future that every community inhabited by them both will be as distinctly divided into two social bodies as if they had no local connection. The two streams will flow side by side, but without intermingling. As the extent of this separation increases, the sympathies that have held the whites and blacks together will weaken, the elements of difference between them only growing more radical, thus revealing very clearly how alien to each other the two peoples are, although dwelling in the same sections of country. The unmistakable tendency is towards a still further diminution of the number of points of general contact between the races ; the only relation of importance between them now is that of employer and employé, but this relation itself implies social isolation, as it is the relation of authority and subordination. The further alienation of the blacks and whites will cause the social customs of the former to approximate still nearer to their special qualities as a people, which signifies a further departure from the spirit of white society. The increase of their population alone will give greater vigor to their distinctive social habits. Even at present, when the whites retain much of their influence over the negroes in a social way, it is obvious that the social life of the latter is animated by very different impulses from that of the former. Being withdrawn more and more to themselves, the social life of the blacks will continue to develop more fully on lines that are peculiar to itself. There are now few elements that are common to the respective societies of the two races —the divergence will be more distinct and rapid in the future, as the longer the period of freedom that has elapsed, the more unique the negroes will become as a people and as a part of the community.

One of the most important results so far of the alienation of the races, is the fact that illicit sexual commerce between them has virtually ceased outside of the towns ; and no circumstances are likely to arise in the future to encourage a renewal of improper intercourse. The only prospect of amalgamation has been through the medium of the female mulattoes, but they are now being rapidly displaced by that class of women who, on account of their temper and appearance, have always been more or less repulsive to the sensibilities of white men. The negroes in the rural communities are fast merging in the original type, which signifies a decline in the number of mulattoes, for the latter show no disposition to create an exclusive circle of their own by intermarriage : on the contrary, they cohabit as readily with the darkest individuals as with men and women of their own shade of color. The tendency of the race to revert, therefore, is increased not only by the reserve of the whites, but by the lack of objection on the part of the mulattoes themselves to sexual intimacy with the blacks. The result of this will be that, in a few generations, the negro of Virginia, wherever he is found in large communities of his own people, will be an exact physical image of his African ancestors.

The return of the race to the original physical type, involves its intellectual reversion also. The alteration in its mental character will be disclosed in the development of simpler and more distinct intellectual traits; with the elimination of the mulattoes, the points of mental difference between the blacks and whites will grow more apparent. So far, the only persons of unusual capacity whom the former race has produced have been men who were sprung, either directly or remotely, from white ancestry. The mental resemblance of negroes to each other will be more notable in the future than it has been in the past, because all are approximating the same type in which they will in time be fully merged, irrespective of difference of origin or of local situation.

The reversion to the original type is apt to make the negro a more dangerous political factor, because it will increase his inability to grasp enlightened ideas of public policy. He will probably sink to a lower plane of political ignorance, and grow still more out of sympathy with the institutions under which he lives. As the social and intellectual gulf between himself and the white people widens, he is likely to fall more completely under the influence of his antipathy to the dominant class; and this, in general, will shape his political action. Bribery, perhaps, will be the only effective means of inducing a large number of his fellows to cast their votes with the whites on important issues, and, in consequence, bribery in one form or another will play a very conspicuous part in all communities where many members of his race are found. The social aspect of negro suffrage is certain to grow more threatening as the blacks increase, inasmuch as this implies their more thorough subjection to those evil influences that emanate from themselves when dwelling together in a mass. The motives that have led the great body of whites to vote together in this age, must augment in force in the age to follow. As a people, there is strong reason to believe that they will not consent to be governed by a horde of ignorant black voters, and in this they will be influenced not so much by sentimental feeling, as by a determination to maintain a stable administration that will fulfil all the needs of society. A reunion will be the final result of every important division in the ranks of the white voters, because the fact that the ballots of the negroes are cast in favor of one side or another, will in the end produce a revulsion of sentiment throughout white society. While many of the whites will always seek to use negro suffrage for the attainment of their own purposes, the triumph of any faction composed of a small minority of white voters and a large majority of the blacks cannot be lasting, inasmuch as that triumph, if prolonged for a considerable length of time, will introduce such disastrous elements of confusion, and foster such embittered antagonism of race, as to be destructive of the coalition. The special bearing of public questions is certain to sink into insignificance as compared with the general bearing of the continued success of the negroes at the polls. The acknowledged issues of all the most important elections will be overshadowed to a great extent by the silent issues raised by the direct conflict of the masses of blacks and whites. It is not improbable that such occasions will be attended with much disorder, arising less from heated political opposition than from passions inflamed by antipathies of race.

Every circumstance surrounding the negro in the present age seems to point directly to his further moral decadence. The numerical expansion of his race will deepen its unfortunate peculiarities, if for no other reason, because that expansion will lead to the complete separation of the blacks and whites, even when dwelling together in the same communities. The decline of the negro in morality will be exactly in proportion to the gradations of his withdrawal from contact with the white people. When the last tradition of slavery has been lost, and the relations between the two races have been readjusted in thorough accord with the conditions of free citizenship, unmodified by any surviving influence of the past, the gulf between them will be far more obvious than it is now. The influences that are shaping the character of the younger generations appear to be such as must bring the blacks in time to a state of nature, so far as a people inhabiting a country where a system of law and government prevails can fall into that state. Situated as they are in communities where the criminal code is enforced, and where all public power is directed by the whites to the support of the continued organization of society, their return to a condition of nature would be observed only in their domestic relations. The drift now is towards a further debasement of all these relations, which is not only indicative of general demoralization, but also promotive of its increase. The probability is that, in a few generations, formal and legal marriages will be much less frequent than they are now, and the promiscuous intercourse between the sexes will grow more open and unreserved. This unrestrained licentiousness would exercise a powerful influence upon the disposition of the children, an influence altogether pernicious and dangerous, which in time would show itself in the further decay of the society of the race.

All search for some means of completely arresting the moral decline of the negro seems to be in vain. There are only two general plans that appear to be in the least likely even to retard it. I have already referred to one of these plans in my remarks on the character of the school system—namely, the erection of normal schools, in which a stringent discipline shall be enforced in the education of students who have stood the severest moral test of selection that the race can endure. The public schools should, if possible, be entirely supplied with men of this stamp, who have been chosen as competent to carry out a special moral rather than a special intellectual mission. Whether a body of negroes, remarkable for their general fitness for a task so delicate and intricate as that which they will have to perform, can be gathered together, is open to considerable doubt, but there can be no question that men thus selected are far better adapted for the work than negroes who have been appointed indiscriminately.

The second plan resembles the first in principle. It is for the white sectarian denominations to establish seminaries in which the best personal material furnished by the race, obtained by as rigid a test as that which should prevail in the normal school, can be prepared to serve as religious missionaries to their people. The graduates of such seminaries should be despatched to the rural communites to labor under the supervision of the organizations that have educated them ; they should be carefully superintended, and their general lives subjected to uninterrupted scrutiny. There is substantial ground for asserting that the missionary efforts of white persons, with a view to the religious improvement of the negroes, will not prove very fruitful in the future, on account of the social separation of the races. All money thus expended, and all energy put forth, will probably be wasted.

The general decline of the blacks in morals can only be arrested even partially by the intervention of the negro himself ; the endeavors of the whites, therefore, should be directed to the proper education of the colored teacher and preacher for the work which circumstances impose upon them alone. If they shall prove themselves to be inefficient or impotent, the last hope of improving the condition of the masses of the race will have been dispelled ; but it is the duty of the State and the Church that such teachers and preachers shall have the most favorable opportunities of testing their competence.

It is a notable fact that the negro appears to most advantage in cities, not only because he is there brought into the closest and most constant contact with white people, but also because he is under the immediate supervision of the police. The moral decline of the race in the rural districts would perhaps be somewhat retarded by the rigid enforcement of the law, even in its smallest details ; every form of crime among them should, for their own welfare, if not for the safety of the community, be severely and swiftly punished, as a general warning. That their lesser offenses are not now punished to the degree that they should be, is due, in some measure, to the fear which the property holder has of exciting their enmity. The planter who would arrest every pilferer among his laborers would undoubtedly run the risk of having his buildings and crops destroyed by incendiary fires, or his cattle secretly poisoned. Apprehension of a similar danger would lurk in his mind with respect to his domestic servants, if he were to bring them to justice for every violation of law, however petty, of which they were guilty.

The increase of crime by the blacks among themselves

is apt to be proportionate only to the growth of their population, with the exception of offenses that spring from superstition, which will be ranker in their communities in the future than it is even now, both because the negroes will be more numerous and because they will be much more withdrawn to themselves. The infractions of law arising in this connection will probably multiply, partially from the fact that the blacks will be inclined to connive at such crimes or will be terrorized into secrecy. All offenses which they can commit against the whites will occur more frequently, as that spirit of subservience which they still feel in their association with the ruling class, in consequence of the recollection or the tradition of slavery, declines with the lapse of years. This is not apt to be observed in the instance of murder or burglary, from which the worst individuals of the race shrink, on account of the personal boldness, coolness, and fortitude which the perpetration of such crimes requires ; it will be much more notable in the case of all criminal acts that can be carried out in a secret and furtive way, without personal danger at the moment to the felon, such as arson, incendiarism, and poisoning. For the same reason, it is highly probable that rape will be committed more often in the future than it has been in the past, in spite of the summary punishment which is meted out to it. While the heinous offenses perpetrated by the negroes will be fewer on the whole than would be expected of a population so little trained in morality and occupying such a low position in the social scale, yet they are always likely to demoralize, to a great extent, the regular and legal administration of the law, for the natural horror which their worst crimes against the white people will excite in the breasts of the latter will be aggravated by antipathies of race, finding vent under the impulse of the moment in deeds of determined violence.

So far as the material condition of the negroes is concerned, they will continue, for several generations, at least, to constitute the principal part of the laboring population of every community in which they dwell ; in fact, it will only be as tillers of the soil that the great body will be employed in the plantation districts, for the mechanical trades are likely, in time, to fall altogether into the hands of white men. Owing to their local situation and their extreme poverty, the blacks will be constrained to work, the force of necessity rather than any desire to improve their condition making them as a people more or less industrious ; but as their only wish will be to supply their immediate wants, they are apt to relax for the time being when this object is temporarily accomplished. They are not likely to cease to be restless, and also unreliable in adhering to their engagements ; but the probability is, that they will not be disposed to disorder labor by turbulent interference unless acting under the influence of white labor organizations. This will be due to the fact that they have no turn for coöperation ; and then, too, they will always be more in the power of the land-owners than the artisans and mechanics of the large cities are in the power of manufacturers. It is true that they also can combine and strike, but their position will be much more precarious, because they can be expelled from their homes as well as discharged—a serious matter if all the planters of the same section are organized.

There is only one contingency that is calculated to destroy the prosperity of the Virginian negro as a laborer in the future, namely, the complete disruption of that system of large farms and plantations which now prevails, especially in the tobacco region, where the black population of the State is principally concentrated. There is apparent in the latter section a tendency towards the breaking up of this system, because agricultural operations there are not profitable, as a rule, when conducted on a considerable scale, on account of the low prices of products, the amount paid in wages to laborers, and also the general unreliability of the laborers themselves. The small farmers and planters are rapidly increasing in number and influence. The drift is towards a still greater division of land and a more general distribution of such property among the white people ; this drift being the source of benefit to a few negroes, who are prudent and economical enough to save their earnings, but to the mass of the race it is an obstacle in the way of their obtaining a subsistence. The existence of a general system of small estates would imply the cultivation of the soil, for the most part, by the families of white proprietors ; in consequence of which there would not be the same demand for the services of the blacks, and any decline in that demand is detrimental to their interests. This will be peculiarly the case in the future, when they have increased very much ; the competition among themselves will then be more active, even if their present advantageous position as laborers were to remain unaffected by an alteration in the system of land-holding. Any change that diminishes the calls upon their manual strength will react injuriously to their fortunes in a pecuniary sense.

So far as the accumulation of property is involved, especially property in the form of land, the progress of the negroes will probably be less marked in the future than it has been in the past. The period of twenty years that has elapsed since the war has offered the fairest opportunities that are ever likely to arise of purchasing estates, and yet the proprietors, even among men who are old enough to to have been trained in the strict and regular school of slavery, are very few as compared with the masses of their people. The numerical disproportion between the proprietors who belong respectively to the older and younger generations is still more significant. The number of colored land-owners will perhaps decrease relatively to the growth of the black population, but the rapidity of this decrease is dependent upon the condition of the various sections of the State. There has already been an advance in the value of the soil in many parts of the tobacco region on account of the demand for land among the members of the class of small planters and farmers. This means that the ability of the negro to buy even a few acres in those parts has been diminished, which has had a tendency to encourage further the extravagance and wastefulness of the race. The growth of prosperity has a blighting influence on their fortunes everywhere, because such prosperity implies, to a certain extent, the greater stringency of the conditions of exist-ence, and any stringency at all has always affected them very injuriously in every way, as they find it impossible, with all their undoubted power of adaptation, to acquire such habits of economy, prudence, and foresight as to learn to adjust themselves to harsh situations. Statistics dis-close that they do not expand numerically in the cities for this reason, and they would not multiply in the country at the present rate if it were not so easy to earn a livelihood.

II.

What is to be the final destiny of the negro, not only in Virginia, but in the tier of great States that lie to the south

and southwest, a vast extent of country where the individuals of his race are remarkable for the same unfortunate qualities and for equally dangerous tendencies. If
there is any happy solution of the problem which the
numerical strength as well as the general disposition of
the blacks creates throughout the Southern division of
the republic, it must be the result of influences now
at work there. The only influences that are likely to
lead to such a solution are those that are breaking up the
system of large farms and plantations which prevailed in
the age of slavery and which has survived to the present
era. The gradual disruption of this system is observed
in every part of the Southern States where the climate is
agreeable to the health of white people ; the only question is as to the degree of progress which it is making
and how far it will proceed, for there can be no doubt
that its inevitable effect, if it shall reach its extreme limit,
will be to check the further expansion of the black population. In the general distribution of land that is now
going on, the negroes, especially those who belong to the
generation that has come of age since the war, are
obtaining only a trivial share, a share that sinks into
peculiar insignificance when the numerical proportion of
the races is recalled. The overwhelming majority of the
Southern blacks must continue to be laborers without
any interest in the soil that they till. It is not improbable, however, that the day will arrive when the salubrious
portion of the South will have been divided into such
small holdings that their white owners will be able to
cultivate them without the need of much assistance.
This would be wholly destructive of the material prosperity of the great body of negroes even as ordinary
working men. But long before this point in the disrup-

tion of the old agricultural system of the South would be reached, a strong pressure would be brought to bear to force the masses of the race back upon the poorest lands, where it would be so difficult to earn a subsistence that the growth of the black population would not only cease, but a decline in its numerical strength would even set in. The inclination of that population from Virginia to Texas under these circumstances, if they should arise in the course of time, would be to drift towards the malarious regions of the Gulf and the lower Mississippi Valley, where it will always be difficult for the whites to live on account of the pestilential nature of the climate. Here the blacks would form large communities, which would become such dangerous elements in the States to which they would belong, that it would be to the interest of the white people to allow the negroes to erect a commonwealth of their own over which they could exercise an absolute control.

The tendency towards the division of the soil in the upland parts of the South will probably be hastened by many influences. In the first place, the members of the white population are not now emigrating to the extent that they formerly did. In the second place, the Southern cities are increasing in size and wealth, which, in time, will have the effect of improving the condition of the rural communities by enhancing the value of land. In the third place, there is a disposition everywhere now to construct railroads by county subscriptions, which always create a number of new industries. And finally, when the West is fully occupied, there will be an inclination on the part of immigrants, Northern as well as foreign, to settle in the South—first in border States like Virginia and Tennessee, and afterwards on the lines of lower sections of country. The fierce competition in the older communities which they abandon will perhaps make them indifferent to the obstacles with which they will have to contend when brought into contact with negroes.[1]

Admitting as true that there is a tendency towards the distribution of land among the whites throughout the greater portion of the South ; admitting further that this tendency must culminate in a system of small estates resembling those observed at the North, which are cultivated by the families of the white proprietors, with some assistance from hired laborers ; admitting all this as substantially correct, or, at least, within the range of probability, we are at once confronted with the various evils that will flow from the growth of the black population in that interval that must elapse before the gradual disruption of the old agricultural system can exercise a marked influence, either in checking the propagation of the negroes, or in forcing them to emigrate to the malarious regions of the Gulf and the Mississippi Valley. For half a century, at least, the blacks of the South will continue to expand numerically at an alarming rate, because, during that period of time, the soil must remain comparatively cheap and abundant, and the negro be in sufficient demand as a laborer to supply him with all that is necessary to his existence. The social and political evils that will accompany this expansion will be as great as if there were no influence in operation to obstruct it in the end ; the temporary posi-

---

[1] All these influences will affect the interests of the negro very unfavorably, for the reason that I have mentioned, namely, they will make the conditions of existence far more stringent than they are now for the race.

tion of the Southern States will be as trying in consequence as if there were no prospect of final relief. However fortunate may be the result of this influence in the distant future, these States must for many decades be surrounded with an increasing number of causes for immediate apprehension.

If time shall show that the tendency towards the division of land among the Southern whites is insignificant in its scope after all, and without an element of permanence, and if the numerical expansion of the blacks shall exclude all those foreign influences that would improve the condition of the South, then it is impossible to regard its future without a feeling of profound misgiving. As long as there are vast spaces unoccupied by the whites and the means of earning a subsistence are so easy, the increase of the black population will be practically unlimited. The unlimited increase of that population is pregnant with innumerable calamities. It virtually means that a period will come when there will be a sharp contest between blacks and whites for the possession of a large part of the Southern States ; and in this contest the whites will not peacefully yield a foot of ground unless they are slowly excluded by the irresistible pressure that will result from an enormous numerical disproportion between the two races. The South cannot remain permanently half black and half white. That section is as radically divided against itself to-day as the Union was when composed of free and slave States ; and the words which Abraham Lincoln quoted then can be quoted with equal aptness now : "No house divided against itself can stand." Either the whites or the negroes must withdraw or be extinguished by the stress of natural influences. The white people are favored by the

fact that they belong to a race that has always been remarkable for intelligence, courage, and an invincible
determination to maintain its supremacy. Furthermore,
they hold possession of the soil. On the other hand,
although the blacks are intellectually and morally deficient, yet they have the strength of numbers that are
multiplying with startling rapidity. All schemes that
contemplate a forcible solution of the problem to the
advantage of the whites are visionary and impracticable.
The deportation to a separate territory of their own, of
the mere annual increase of the negroes, would throw the
whole South into bankruptcy. The acquisition of a
settled country like San Domingo, with a view to the
encouragement of immigration thither by national subsi-
dies, although perfectly feasible, would hardly be accep-
table to the national judgment. There does not seem to
be any substantial ground for anticipating that the public
schools will solve the problem by imparting to the masses
of the blacks a just conception of the duties and responsibilities of citizenship, thus finally assimilating them as
a people to the spirit of our institutions. This opinion
is based upon a close observation of the operation
of the school system in one State only, but the negroes
are so homogeneous everywhere, the general influences
throughout the South are so similar, that what is true of
the race in one commonwealth is apt to be true of its
members in a great division of country and as one distinct people. Even admitting that the public schools
can meet and remove all the dangers of the situation,
there is every prospect that the growth of the black population will be so rapid and enormous that the resources
of the Union would in a century be unable to satisfy
its educational needs. The first conspicuous influence

of instruction will be to cause the negroes to be restive under the deprivation of power proportionate to their numbers. In making the blacks more clearly aware of their numerical strength, it will inspire them with a desire to use it with a view to their own aggrandizement; but no instance that history furnishes of the domination of the race leads us to believe that its members are competent to direct an enlightened system of administration. Wherever on the face of the globe negroes have established commonwealths of their own, they have shown themselves to be wholly incapable of self-government. In Hayti, where they have had the fairest field for the experiment, for it is an island that combines every variety of soil and climate, disorder and revolution have prevailed without intermission since they declared their independence. There they are rapidly reverting to the African tribal relations. Human bodies are secretly sold in the markets of the capital city for meat, and the highest officers of the State are involved in the cannabalistic practices of the Voudoo sect, which are encouraged and participated in by the great body of the people. The queen of the Antilles, the most beautiful island in the world, has virtually become a savage jungle.[1]

Jamaica has sunk to an equally hopeless condition. One of the fairest parts of the globe, a part upon which nature has lavished without stint her greatest treasures and beauties, has declined to a tropical wilderness far more wretched, with its evidences of a former prosperity, than when the foot of Columbus first touched the shores of San Salvador. Africa, the most fertile of all the con-

[1] See the temperate, able, and interesting work of Sir Spencer St. John, late British Consul to Hayti, entitled : " Hayti, or the Black Republic," and published as recently as 1884.

tinents, and upon its central plateaus one of the most
salubrious, with magnificent lakes and streams that offer
a network of highways to internal commerce, is observed
to-day, when the arts have been carried to the highest
pitch of development elsewhere, to be the scene of the
lowest forms of barbarism and the home of the most degraded types of humanity. But the strongest proof that
can be furnished of the unfortunate qualities of the
negro is to be found in the history of the South during the
period of reconstruction, when he reduced many illustri-
ous commonwealths to political chaos and brought society itself to the verge of ruin. That a race which has
occupied such a large portion of the globe should in all
ages and under the most favorable circumstances have
shown itself to be so incapable not only of creating civilization, but also of preserving its fruits when introduced
to a civilization not their own, must be due to the want
of those virtues and vigorous elements of character that
have distinguished every people who have played an
important part in the affairs of the world.

The same deficiencies that render the negro unable to
govern cause his influence to be highly dangerous, even
when he is a subordinate political factor. For this reason the expression, the solid South, has no sectional significance ; it merely embodies the determination of the
whites to ward off political ruin and to save society from
destruction. There are no fundamental differences in
popular feeling, because such differences are radically
inconsistent not only with the welfare of the community,
but even with its permanent existence. The discussion
and agitation of questions of national concern have already ceased in the Southern States, inasmuch as all divergence of political opinion involves social anarchy in

the conclusion. Not until the negro is eliminated as a political factor will the equilibrium of the Union be restored, for not until then will the Southern whites separate into parties. They were bound together before the war by a common interest in the maintenance of the institution of slavery ; they are united in sentiment now by the evils incident to negro suffrage, and they will remain united as long as the blacks enjoy as a mass the right to vote. If that right were curtailed, the Southern people would be more evenly divided between parties than the citizens of the North are to-day. As it is, the future, so far from extending any promise that the solidarity of the Southern States will be broken, offers still weightier reasons why that solidarity shall be preserved—reasons springing from the numerical expansion of the black population, which will certainly continue to grow during the course of several generations, if not for a practically indefinite time. Negro suffrage has compelled the South to assume an eminently conservative attitude with respect to her own affairs, and this conservatism will deepen with her increasing difficulties and dangers. To withdraw from her present policy is to relegate her institutions, social as well as political, to anarchy and barbarism ; but to pursue that policy for a great length of time would seem to be impossible. It is doubtful whether any country can thrive that must permanently remain in the condition of an armed camp. The partial disfranchisement of the negro in the future would appear to be inevitable as essential, if not to the existence of the South, then to the prosperity of the Union.

The questions raised by the presence of the negro have always been the most perplexing in our national life, and from the beginning the American people have deferred the settlement of these questions until they became too pressing to be evaded. First, there was the acrimonious wrangle as to the extension of slavery, which finally culminated in one of the most sanguinary and fratricidal of wars. This was followed by the bestowal of the franchise on the freedman, which shook all the institutions of the Southern States to their lowest foundations ; and to-day the rapid increase of the black population constitutes a graver danger to the stability of our government than any that is sapping the vitality of the European monarchies. During all of the later periods of our national history the majestic and radiant figure of the Republic has been dogged by the ominous shadow of the negro—now as a slave, stripped of every privilege, and now as a citizen, holding aloft the ballot in his hand. In the course of the next ten decades American institutions will be subjected to a severer strain than they have yet endured, and one of the most important causes of this strain will be the evil influence which the Southern blacks will indirectly exercise on the national destiny, an influence that time will only make more pernicious if nothing shall intervene to check their numerical growth. The negro is only useful to the Southern States, and through those States to the Union, as a laborer, but it would be far better for the whole country if he were withdrawn, even though withdrawn so suddenly as to wholly blight, for a time, the material interests of the South. It would be better, indeed, for that entire section to be relegated to its primeval condition with a view to its being settled again exclusively by a white population, just as if it were a virgin territory, than for it to maintain its present position partially through the manual exertions of the blacks, but with the individuals of that race increasing so rapidly as to threaten the extinction in the end of every element of prosperity, with no hope of subsequent revival.

The position of the South with respect to the negro problem should not be misunderstood. Its proper solution is a matter of profound solicitude to her from whatever standpoint it may be viewed. Thousands of her citizens, whose patriotism is coextensive with the republic, are deeply and constantly meditating on the dangers of her situation and speculating as to how these dangers can be removed. The questions involved have risen above the plane of antipathies of race. They have passed from the sphere of individuals and parties. They now bear alone upon the final destinies of a great section of country, endowed by the Creator with every advantage of climate and soil, a section capable of supporting a teeming population and suited to become the scene of the highest development of American civilization. Fervent should be the prayer that the course of future events will solve this momentous problem at last in a way that will redound to the prosperity of the South and the glory of the Union. In the meanwhile the Southern people are using every means in their reach to bring about this consummation, and upon the efforts that they have made and are still making with that view they may well invoke, in the language of the Emancipation Proclamation that precipitated the special evils that now environ them, " the considerate judgment of mankind and the gracious favor of Almighty God."